TRADITIONAL COUNTRY LIFE RECIPE SERIES

ICE CREAM
THE ULTIMATE
COLD COMFORT

TRADITIONAL COUNTRY LIFE RECIPE SERIES

ICE CREAM
THE ULTIMATE
COLD COMFORT

by Jeri Quinzio

Interior illustrations by
Jeri Quinzio

Cover illustration by
Lisa Adams

The Brick Tower Press ®
1230 Park Avenue, New York, NY 10128
Copyright © 2006 by Jeri Quinzio

All rights reserved under the International and Pan-American Copyright Conventions.
Printed in the United States by J. T. Colby & Company, Inc., New York.
No part of this publication may be reproduced, stored in a retrieval system, or transmitted in any form or by any means, electronic, mechanical, photocopying, recording, or otherwise, without the prior written permission of the publisher.

Quinzio, Jeri
The Traditional Country Life Recipe Series:
Includes Index
ISBN-13: 978-1-883283-36-0
ISBN-10: 1-883283-36-1, softcover

Library of Congress Catalog Card
Number: 2006933840
First Edition, November 2006

TABLE OF CONTENTS

The Story of Ice Cream

Cold Comfort.....3

America Discovers Ice Cream....9

The Ices Age....12

Sipping Sodas....16

Ice Cream Goes to War....20

Ice Cream at the Millenium...24

Recipes

Making Ice Cream......25

Ice Creams......29

Frozen Mousses........68

Sorbets.........72

Granita........87

Sauces.........91

Simple Servings & Toppings...95

Index.....102

Dedication

This book is dedicated to the memory of my father, Nick Quinzio, who tasted, and even more important, seriously critiqued my ices and ice creams.

Acknowledgements

I am also grateful to the many others without whom this book would not exist. They include:

The members of my writing workshop: Myrna Kaye, Roberta Leviton, Barbara Mende, Sabra Morton, Shirley Moskow, Beth Surdut, Molly Turner, Rose Yesu, and the late Doris Pullen.

The Culinary Historians of Boston, in particular Barbara Haber, Pat Kelly, Joyce Toomre, and Barbara K. Wheaton.

My foodie friends, my family, and my husband, Dan Coleman, who never met an ice cream he didn't like.

COLD COMFORT
by Jeri Quinzio

The discovery of a new dish does more for human happiness than the discovery of a star, the noted gourmet Brillat-Savarin once wrote. If that's so, the discovery of ice cream must be worth a whole galaxy. And the name of the discoverer should be emblazoned in the heavens.

The trouble is, we don't know who made that first dish of vanilla, strawberry, or triple chocolate chunk ice cream. That may explain why there are candidates for the honor all over the world.

Some give the ancient Romans credit for inventing ice cream, but although they did send their slaves off to the mountains to get snow, they didn't make ice cream with it. They poured syrup on it and ate it, or they used it to chill their wines or fruit.

Others say Marco Polo brought ice cream back to Italy from China. He didn't. The Chinese and the Europeans developed their ice creams separately.

In the Arab world, snow and ice were combined with fruits and a sweetener -- usually honey or sugar -- to make a chilled drink called a *sharbât*. The word led to the English sherbet, the French *sorbet*, the Italian *sorbetto* and the Spanish *sorbete*. But a *sharbât* was and still is a drink.

The most-told story is that Catherine de Medici brought ices from Italy to France in the 16th century when she married the future king Henry II. The reality is that ices didn't appear in France for another century, and French confectioners said they had to go to Italy to learn how to make them.

Ices and ice creams probably were developed in Italy. In the 16th century, Italian scientists experimenting with freezing learned how to intensify the cold of natural ice by mixing it with salt. Their experiments inspired confectioners to try transforming their icy drinks and cool custards into ices and ice creams.

At first, there was a lot of skepticism about eating ices or ice creams. Some physicians thought it was unnatural and dangerous, and blamed it for everything from colic to paralysis. Others countered that ices cured diseases, especially scurvy, emaciation, and paralysis. Clearly those doctors had a bigger following.

In 1694, Antonio Latini wrote the first Italian cookbook with recipes for ices. He didn't claim to be an innovator, though. In fact, he wrote, "Everyone in Naples is born knowing how to make ice cream."

M.Emy, *L'art de bein faire les glaces d'office* (Paris, 1768) Courtesy, The Winterthur Library: Printed Book and Periodical Collection

But it's clear that his were early recipes. For one thing, Latini listed snow and salt among his ingredients. In later books, they were mentioned only as part of the freezing instructions. Latini's recipes for ices are listed under the heading: "Of various sorts of ices and frozen waters." The earliest ices were, in fact, frozen versions of popular drinks. Interspersed among his recipes for waters, Latini had recipes for lemon, chocolate, cherry and cinnamon ices, as well as an ice made with milk and candied citron or pumpkin.

Most early 18th century cookbook authors didn't even write separate recipes for ices. They just introduced the section on drinks by saying that to turn drinks into ices, one should double the sugar and the flavoring, then freeze. They knew that a mixture that's just right at room temperature lacks flavor when it's frozen. Lemon, strawberry, red currant, pomegranate, pistachio, cinnamon, and fennel were all popular flavors, first for iced drinks and then for ices.

Custards and creams were among the favorite desserts on 18th century tables, and cooks made them in every flavor imaginable. Rose petals, raspberries, ginger, lemon, musk, caramel, tea, chervil, tarragon, celery, and bay leaves were all stirred first into creams and then into ice creams. That's why, early on, ice creams were often called "iced creams" or "cream ices."

The earliest recipes generally devoted more space to the perils and pitfalls of freezing than they did to the formulas for the ice cream -- with good reason. Freezing wasn't easy before refrigeration. Here's how it worked: After cooks figured out the correct proportion and type of salt to mix with the ice or snow, they put it all into a large pail. Then they mixed up their ice cream recipe and poured it into a smaller freezing pot called a *sorbetière*, stirred it and covered the pot tightly. They put the *sorbetière* into the ice-and-salt-filled pail carefully, to make sure no salt or water got into it, and banked the ice up around it to begin the freezing process.

Cooks soon learned that if they didn't stir and shake the mixture while it was freezing, the resulting ice cream would have icicles. So from time to time they had to take the *sorbetière* out, open it, and scrape the sides and bottom of the pot to incorporate all the frozen bits into the rest of the mixture. Then they stirred it. Next, they resealed the cover and put the pot back into the pail, again being careful that no salt or water got into it. They shook the pot frequently to keep the mixture moving and repeated the opening, scraping, stirring, sealing procedure several times. The freezing pot also had to be drained occasionally as the ice melted. The process took hours.

When the ice cream was ready, cooks would either serve it or put it in a decorative mold and store it in an icebox, until they were ready to unmold and serve it. Or, instead of molding it, they could leave the ice cream in the *sorbetière* until serving time. Either way, it had to be surrounded with ice and salt to keep it from melting. No wonder it was an elite treat, made by professional confectioners or reserved for those who could afford a kitchen staff.

Despite the tediousness of making it, ice cream became all the rage in Europe. In 1768, M. Emy wrote the first book devoted to the subject, *"L'Art de bien faire les glaces d'office,"* for professional confectioners.

Emy weighed in on the health question, conceding that eating too much ice cream might cause colic. However, he also believed people got sick when they didn't have enough ice cream. This may not have been a completely unbiased position for the author of an ice cream cookbook.

Emy offered recipes for dozens of ices and ice creams, mostly delectable ones like apricot, caramel, and raspberry. However, he also made oddities like an ice cream flavored with Parmesan and Gruyère cheeses and another with truffles -- the fungi, not the chocolates. He wasn't alone in making unusual, even bizarre, ice creams. One of his contemporaries made artichoke ice cream, and the great French chef Escoffier made a pureed asparagus ice cream.

In his book, Emy gave detailed instructions for molding and painting ice creams to look like everything from bunches of bananas to fuzzy peaches, a popular practice at the time. He served orange and lemon ices in the hollowed-out fruits, walnut ice cream in walnut shells, and fruit ices on fresh fruit leaves or branches. He wrote that previous generations didn't make ices properly, but that they were now *"parfaites."*

AMERICA DISCOVERS ICE CREAM

Europeans impressed dinner guests with displays of ices molded and painted to imitate other foods. Americans were impressed by simple bowls of ice cream. A guest of Thomas Jefferson at Monticello wrote that Jefferson served "Ice cream, very good; a dish somewhat like pudding."

America's first families were big ice cream fans. George Washington bought a "Cream Machine for Making Ice" in May, 1784. Dolley Madison was so famous for serving ice cream that an ice cream company was named after her. Thomas Jefferson's papers included his own handwritten recipe for vanilla ice cream which, it is thought, he picked up on a trip to France. Jefferson was a tireless collector of recipes for dishes he'd tried and liked.

Jefferson's ice cream:
2 bottles of good cream
6 yolks of eggs
1/2 pound of sugar
mix the yolks & sugar
put the cream on a fire in a casserole, first putting in a stick of Vanilla.
when near boiling take it off & pour it gently into the mixture of eggs & sugar.
stir it well.
put it on the fire again stirring it thoroughly with a spoon to prevent its sticking to the casserole.
when near boiling take it off and strain it thro' a towel.
put it in the Sabottiere. [sic]

This was followed by detailed instructions for freezing. Except that Jefferson did not say how big the bottles of "good cream" were, his recipe is very similar to today's.

Americans who lived in urban areas and could afford it bought ice cream from fashionable confectioners. On May 12, 1777 an ad in the *New York Gazette* stated that "Philip Lenzi, Confectioner from London" had ice cream available "almost every day." Most confectioners offered a few standard flavors and would make others to order.

The Virginia House-wife by Mary Randolph, published in 1824, provided a dozen recipes for ice cream and instructions for freezing and serving. Randolph directed that: "When ice creams are not put into shapes [molds], they should always be served in glasses with handles." Her recipes included vanilla, raspberry, almond, lemon, quince, chocolate and, I'm sorry to say, oyster. This wasn't sweetened; it was oyster soup, strained and frozen.

Not everyone in America was making or even tasting ice cream in the 18th or early 19th century. Ice wasn't always available or affordable, nor was cream. The first American cookbook, *American Cookery* by Amelia Simmons, published in 1796, didn't have any ice cream recipes. Even Jefferson, a man not known for making do, wrote that butter could be creamed and mixed with milk as a substitute for cream. As late as the 1850s, some recipes called for "milk or cream when you have it," or explained how to enrich a milk mixture with eggs or arrowroot so it would be almost as good as cream. Desserts made from beaten egg whites mixed with fruit were called "palatable" ice cream substitutes. Sugar was also very expensive. Most important, making ice cream was so labor-intensive that most people couldn't afford the time. Of course, that wasn't a problem for wealthy slave owners in the South. Harriet Martineau, an English writer who traveled in the U.S. from 1834 to 1836, wrote that at plantations she was served extravagant meals and "to crown the whole, large blocks of ice-cream." However, when she stayed at a modest cabin at White Sulphur Springs, Virginia, she got ice cream that "seemed to be thin custard, with a sprinkling of snow in it."

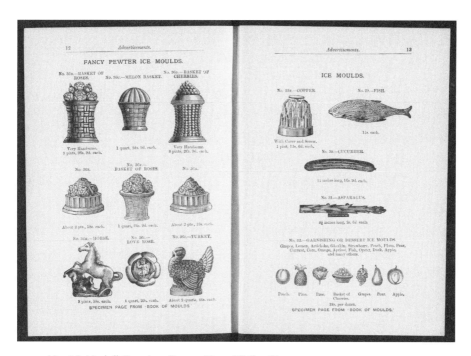

Mrs. A.B. Marshall, *Fancy Ices*   Courtesy, Harvard College Library

THE ICES AGE

American food changed dramatically in the late 19th and early 20th centuries. Refrigeration, mechanized production methods and new forms of transportation transformed the way food was grown, produced, stored and distributed. This was good news for ice cream makers. New refining methods brought the price of sugar down to the point that in 1898, according to home economist Maria Parloa, "the best sugar is so reasonable that there is no necessity for even poor people to seek a cheap grade." New methods also made ice more accessible. Henry David Thoreau wrote, in 1854, that on a good day ice harvesters could chop a thousand tons of ice from a single pond near Boston, Massachusetts.

Ice cream-making equipment improved, too. Thomas Masters, an Englishman, invented an ice cream maker primarily intended for professionals in 1843. Nancy Johnson, an American, invented one suitable for home use in 1846. Johnson's featured a crank and a dasher inside the freezing pot so that the ice cream mixture could be stirred without taking the freezing pot out of the pail and opening it. Her new freezer made the job much easier for home cooks. Other improvements soon followed.

Jacob Fussell, a Baltimore dairyman, became the first ice cream wholesaler in America in 1851. He had been running a dairy business, buying milk from small farms in the Pennsylvania Dutch countryside near the Northern Central

An enterprising confectioner. Image courtesy of Historic New England, Boston.

Pennsylvania town, packed the country-fresh ice cream in ice, and sent it to Baltimore via the train. Eventually Fussell opened factories in Baltimore, Washington, Boston and New York. Other wholesalers followed and when the Civil War ended, the ice cream manufacturing business expanded rapidly.

Individual confectioners found it hard to compete with wholesalers who could easily undersell them. The *Confectioners' Journal* of 1883 described the wholesalers as "Cheap-John factorymen," and their products as "frothy, watery slop and slush and still viler 'flavorings,' whose make up is only known to the devil's chemical emissaries."

Ice cream was becoming a mass market product. In 1859, according to today's dairy industry sources, national production was estimated at 4,000 gallons. Ten years later, it was 24,000 gallons. By the turn of the century, despite the fact that it was still mostly a summertime treat, Americans were gobbling up five million gallons a year.

Ice cream appeared on dinner menus at home and in restaurants. It teamed up with cake at birthday parties. Specialized ice cream forks, knives, spoons and dishes all become fashionable. On city streets, vendors screamed "ice cream" and kids came running, pennies clutched in their hands. At stylish new restaurants in New York, unescorted ladies could eat ice cream in public without ruining their reputations. In Paris, eating ices was the height of chic. Author Jules Janin wrote: "At eleven o'clock in the evening, the Café Tortoni is no longer a place for eating, it is a saloon for sherbet and ices…The most elegant beauties, and the most agreeable young men hasten to this last rendezvous…for Tortoni's, they abandon the unfinished Opera: they leave the theatre before the last stab."

The health issue still popped up from time to time. In *A Treatise on Domestic Economy*, published in 1847, Miss Catherine Beecher said eating small amounts of ice cream was acceptable sometimes, but not after meals. She wrote: "Indulging in large quantities of cold drinks, or eating ice-creams, after a meal, tends to reduce the temperature of the stomach, and thus to stop digestion."

Still, ice cream recipes proliferated in American cookbooks and magazines. *Godey's Ladies' Book*, the most popular women's magazine in the 1860s, considered ice cream a necessity and published many "receipts" for it. Mrs. D. A. Lincoln, author of *The Boston Cook Book*, wrote a booklet called *Frozen Dainties* for the White Mountain Freezer Co., a manufacturer of ice cream makers, in 1889. It had 31 recipes, detailed freezing and molding instructions and bits of advice such as: "Remember that an ice-cream freezer will not bear neglect. All machinery needs to be kept well oiled," and "A gallon freezer will freeze a quart, but a quart freezer will not freeze a gallon."

Lincoln's booklet included "Five Receipts for the Foundation of all Ice-cream." The richest, "Neapolitan Ice-cream," was made with both eggs and cream. "Philadelphia Ice-cream" was made with cream but without eggs. "Ice-cream, with Gelatine" used gelatin as a thickener. "Plain Ice-cream" was thickened with flour. Finally, her "Frozen Custard" was made with milk and eggs rather than cream, although she said it would be "greatly improved by adding a little cream." Her pineapple ice cream recipe called for the Philadelphia-style base along with grated pineapple and lemon and orange juices. Her maraschino ice cream was made with the Neapolitan flavored with vanilla, rose, and almond extracts with Maraschino liqueur poured over it. She added macaroons, brown bread crumbs, cold Indian pudding crumbs, and various nuts to her ice creams. Typically, she either ground the additions very fine or steeped them in the mixture for flavor, then strained them out. People then preferred silky smooth ice creams, not our crunchy chunky ones.

This was the heyday of ices served as palate cleansers between dinner courses or as accompaniments to the meat or fish course. In *Frozen Puddings and Desserts*, published in 1913, Mrs. Sarah Rorer recommended serving cucumber sorbet with boiled cod. Her gooseberry sorbet was perfect for "Christmas dinner with goose," and a ginger water ice went with roasted or braised beef. She made a spicy, Bloody-Mary-like tomato sorbet, without alcohol, and served it "in punch glasses at dinner as an accompaniment to roasted beef, or venison, or saddle of mutton." The tomato sorbet was made without any sugar, but most of the others were as sweet as any dessert ice.

SIPPING SODAS

When soda fountains made their debut early in the 19th century, they were more like bars than ice cream shops. They served both alcoholic and soft drinks, and were so male-dominated that eventually some opened separate areas for ladies. As the temperance movement gathered support, most soda fountain operators dropped alcohol and turned their fountains into wholesome hangouts for everyone in the family.

Initially, soda fountains served sodas and they served ice cream, but they didn't serve ice cream sodas. During the 1870s, someone – accounts vary as to exactly who, exactly where – was making a soda that called for ice, flavored syrup, soda water and cream when he ran out of cream. Or the cream soured. At any rate, he substituted ice cream for the cream and created the ice cream soda. It became such a success and so widespread that in 1893 one American magazine called the ice cream soda "Our national beverage."

Nevertheless, some preachers decided it was sinful to sip sodas on Sundays, which led an enterprising soda jerk to invent the sundae. That's how the story goes and it could even be true, although it's more likely that the sundae was invented when a fountain ran out of soda water. Other ice cream innovations followed. Eskimo pies, Good Humor bars, Popsicles, Creamsicles, Fudgsicles and ice cream sandwiches were among the successful ones.

Then there's the ice cream cone, which was invented at the 1904 World's Fair in St. Louis. Or was it? Long before then, European confectioners made wafers and rolled them into cones. They dipped the cones, or cornets as they were also called, into meringue and sprinkled almonds or pistachios on them. They filled them with flavored whipped creams and topped them off with strawberries, and they served them alongside ices. Shortly before the start of the 20th century, Mrs. Agnes Marshall, a British cook and author, wrote that "cornets can also be filled with any cream or water ice…and served for a dinner, luncheon, or supper dish." These were ice cream cones on a silver platter, eaten with a fork and knife, not licked outdoors on a summer day. But they were ice cream cones.

According to the World's Fair story, a vendor selling ice cream in small glass dishes known as penny licks or licking glasses couldn't wash dishes fast enough to keep up with the demand. Ernest Hamwi, a vendor selling wafers, came to his aid. Hamwi rolled the wafers into cone shapes and filled them with ice cream.

Before long, everyone at the fair was eating the ice cream cones he claimed to have invented. Nearly a year before, however, Italo Marchiony, who sold lemon ices from a pushcart in New York, had applied for a patent on a mold that turned out ten cones at a time. He had been making cones by hand and wanted to speed up the process. No matter who first put ice cream in a cone, it was an inspired combination, and the marriage has been a long and happy one.

When Prohibition came along, some danced the Charleston and drank bathtub gin in speakeasies. Others ate ice cream. During the Roaring Twenties, the local soda fountain or ice cream parlor took the place of the corner saloon. It seemed as if everyone in America was bellying up to the ice cream bar. Anheuser-Busch and other breweries switched from producing beer to making ice cream.
"I scream, you scream, we all scream for ice cream!" was a popular song lyric as

well as a kids' rhyme. Ice cream consumption went up by more than 100 million gallons during Prohibition, only beginning to go down with its repeal and the start of the Depression.

The return of legal drinking combined with the Depression hit ice cream makers hard. One of the ways they tried to make up lost ground was by advertising ice cream for breakfast. "Serve it over your cereal in place of cream," suggested one

ad. Ice cream novelties that sold for a nickel, like the Twin-Popsicle and the Side-Walk Sundae, probably did more to help the industry recover, as did celebrity endorsements. The Barrymores, Babe Ruth and Charlie Chaplin all said they were ice cream fans, and President Franklin D. Roosevelt claimed he ate ice cream at least once a day.

By the late 30s, ice cream was having its biggest boom ever. New manufacturing and refrigeration methods changed the business. Instead of old-fashioned ice and salt mixtures, brine and, later, ammonia were used to freeze ice cream. Ice cream could be produced in a continuous stream instead of separate batches, making it possible to turn out more of it faster than ever. Although most people either made their own ice cream or ate it at soda fountains or ice cream parlors, packaged ice cream sales started to increase. Grocers began installing refrigerated cabinets that kept ice cream frozen, and householders started replacing their iceboxes with shiny new refrigerators complete with tiny freezer compartments. Packaged ice cream wouldn't gain significant market share until after the war, but the trend had begun.

ICE CREAM GOES TO WAR

During World War II, the government deemed ice cream a necessity for U.S. fighting forces. It was easy to digest, nutritious and, most important, great for morale. The Navy launched a floating ice cream parlor in the western Pacific, and the Army supplied the troops with enough ingredients to make 80 million gallons a year. In 1943, the U.S. Armed Forces was the world's largest ice cream manufacturer. When the government didn't give soldiers ice cream-making equipment, they made their own – from abandoned motors, shell cases, whatever they could scavenge. Airmen put containers of ice cream mixture in the rear gunners' compartments where planes' vibrations and the intense cold at high altitudes churned and froze the ice cream. Dessert was ready when they landed.

Ice cream played a role on the home front, too, although food shortages and rationing made it a rare treat. In New England, the H.P. Hood Company filled its Hoodsie ice cream cups with vanilla and orange sherbet instead of vanilla and chocolate because cocoa was scarce. Both Hoodsies and Dixie cup lids featured pictures of planes, tanks and guns. Kids collected and traded them, just as they'd collected lids with movie star photos. Grownups paid an extra 10 cents for Victory Sundaes because each one came with a war stamp. Ice cream joined apple pie, not just for dessert, but as a symbol of America.

After the war, gas rationing ended and Americans took to the road. They drove to roadside stands like Dairy Queen, Carvel, and Tastee Freeze and tasted the new soft-serve ice creams, and they stopped at Howard Johnson's for ice cream cones. Johnson had opened his first ice cream stand in 1925 with just three flavors of old-fashioned, hand-cranked ice cream – vanilla, chocolate, and strawberry. By the 50s, building his orange-roofed restaurants even faster than he added flavors, he had 400 restaurants and 28 flavors. Later, Baskin-Robbins would come up with 31 flavors, one for every day of the month. Neighborhood ice cream sellers didn't do as well after the war. The traditional ice cream parlor and the drugstore soda fountain couldn't compete with the chains and large-scale manufacturers. The ice cream parlor became a museum piece in 1955 when one opened at Disneyland.

The neighborhood grocer also faced tough competition. Americans began going to supermarkets, buying packaged ice cream and storing it in their new freezers. Supermarket ice cream was cheap and readily available; it just wasn't very good.

Before the war, the butterfat content of regular ice cream was about 14%. Manufacturers lowered it to 10% during the war, and most kept it there afterwards. They made their ice cream with artificial colors and imitation flavors, and whipped in a lot of air, called "overrun" in industry-speak.

When the older generation talked about how wonderful ice cream used to taste, they weren't just being nostalgic. Some families still made ice cream once in a while, but most did not. As a result, the younger generation of Americans grew up thinking ice cream was an innocuous-tasting mixture of maltodextrin, polysorbate 65, mono and diglycerides, alginate, propylene glycol, guar gum, carboxymethylcellulose and other unpronounceable ingredients all puffed up with air and stuffed into a cardboard box.

In 1960, ice cream maker Reuben Mattus decided he'd rather switch to a different kind of ice cream than fight the high-volume manufacturers who dominated the supermarket business. Mattus created a high-fat, superpremium ice cream he named Häagen-Dazs for its pseudo-European sound and gourmet appeal. The ice cream was made without preservatives and without a lot of air. It came in just three flavors – vanilla, chocolate, and coffee. Mattus discovered that consumers who were starved for rich, high-quality ice cream were willing to pay a lot more for it.

In the summer of 1973, equipped with a five-gallon, motorized White Mountain freezer, Steve Herrell opened an ice cream shop in Somerville, Massachusetts. Herrell pioneered the practice of smooshing brand-name candies and cookies into his high-quality, 14% butterfat ice cream. As customers watched, the scoopers mixed smashed-up Heath bars, Reese's Peanut Butter Cups or Oreo cookies into servings of ice cream. Both the ice cream and the add-ins were so popular that people happily stood in a line that was often several blocks long to get into Steve's. Soon, Ben & Jerry's and other packaged ice cream makers were inspired to make premium ice creams with all kinds of chunky add-ins. Ice cream lovers ate them up.

ICE CREAM AT THE MILLENIUM

At the turn of the twenty-first century, Americans were eating 23 quarts of ice cream per person, per year, more than any other country. Vanilla was America's favorite flavor, with chocolate coming in second. The health issues associated with ice cream were no longer colic and cold stomachs; they were fat and cholesterol. Nevertheless, premium and superpremium ice cream sales were growing, and low-fat ice cream sales were shrinking. Manufacturers were researching the possibility of adding Omega-3 fatty acids to ice cream to give it the health benefits associated with salmon.

With all the premium ice creams on the market today, why make your own? Because it's easy and it's fun. You don't need ice and salt for today's ice cream makers, and they're affordable and simple to use. You control the ingredients so you know exactly what's in your ice cream. No guar gum or salmon required. You can use your imagination, experiment with flavors and add your own chunky bits. You, like Emy, can make ice cream that's *parfaite*.

MAKING ICE CREAM

Making ice cream is fun and, especially after you've done it a few times, it's easy. However, there are a few things to keep in mind.

FREEZING

First, read the instructions that came with your ice cream maker. Every brand is a bit different, and you'll get the best results if you follow the manufacturer's directions. If yours has a canister that needs to be frozen, it really needs to be frozen. I store my canister in the freezer, so I'm always ready to make ice cream. If you can't spare the space all the time, make sure you put it in the freezer at least 24 hours before you plan to use it. Then shake it to make sure it's frozen. If you hear the liquid swishing around inside, it's not. Put it back in the freezer for a few hours. It's also better to chill your ice cream mixture in the refrigerator overnight before you churn it.

However, if your freezing tub or your mixture wasn't quite cold enough and your mixture is still soft after you've churned it for the amount of time suggested by the manufacturer, don't worry. Just put it in a plastic container in the freezer. It'll firm up. I seldom serve my ice cream as soon as it's churned. I think the texture is better when it has a few hours to ripen.

If you're storing the ice cream longer, make sure it's tightly covered so no moisture gets into it. I press plastic wrap over the ice cream before putting the cover on the container.

Don't forget to label your ice cream, especially if you're making lots. You don't want to have to open the containers to see which is which. Opening a container, whether to check on the contents or serve it, makes ice crystals form. I usually store a quart of ice cream in two pint-size containers so I don't have to keep opening and scooping from one larger container.

Homemade ice cream is better than store-bought in every way but one. With no preservatives, it doesn't keep as long. After a week or so, it loses flavor. However, it tastes so good that keeping it is seldom an issue.

THE MIXTURE

Here are a few hints about making your ice cream mixture. If you've never made ice cream before, you might want to start with one that doesn't contain eggs. Try Marmalade, Chocolate Spice, or Banana Daiquiri ice cream. Biscuit Tortoni is super-easy. Or start with some simple sorbets.

However, if you're making a custard-style ice cream and the custard curdles, don't panic. Just strain it. The next time, take it a little slower. Enjoy the process. Watch the mixture as you stir it. Notice the subtle changes in texture and even color as it begins to thicken. Soon, you'll get to the point where you'll recognize the signs, the sounds and the scents. You'll know when to take the pan off the stove, and pour the mixture into the clean bowl that's ready and waiting. After a couple of tries, you'll be a custard pro.

DETAILS

In any recipe that calls for fruit peel, use only the zest. The zest is the peel minus the white pith under it, which tends to be bitter.

Toasting nuts before adding them to ice cream keeps them crisper and brings out their flavor.

Some of the recipes contain alcohol, and it is not cooked off.

These recipes make roughly a quart, depending on your ice cream maker. If you wind up with a little more, the extra is a designated cook's snack.

THE BOTTOM LINE

The most important thing to remember is that this is ice cream. It's not life or death. If you use five eggs instead of six, or forget to add the almond extract, or don't chill your freezing tub long enough, the world will still turn. And the ice cream will, in all probability, still taste great.

Thornton Wilder wrote: "Enjoy your ice cream while it is on your plate."
I hope you'll enjoy making it as much as eating it.

ALMOND ICE CREAM SMOOTH OR CRUNCHY

NOTE: SMOOTH, *this is a wonderfully subtle ice cream for layering in cakes, meringues. Try the CRUNCHY option for more texture. Either way, it's excellent paired with raspberry ice cream*

(1) Toast the almonds just enough to bring out their flavor, but don't let them brown.
(2) Cool, then put them in a food processor or blender with 1/3 cup of the sugar, and grind until fine.
(3) Warm the milk in a saucepan, stir in the almond-sugar mixture, and bring almost to a boil.
(4) Remove from heat, cover, and let the mixture steep for 15 minutes or so.
(5) Half fill a large bowl or saucepan with ice or ice water and set aside.
(6) Mix the egg yolks and sugar in another saucepan and whisk until thick and pale.
(7) Strain almond and milk mixture and then stir a little of it into the egg mixture. Gradually stir in the rest until it's all combined.
(8) Pour the mixture into a clean bowl, and set that bowl in the one containing the ice. Be careful not to let any ice or water get into the ice cream mixture.
(9) Stir in the cream, almond extract and salt.
(10) Stir occasionally until cooled.
(11) Cover with plastic wrap pressed against surface to prevent a skin forming on top.
(12) Chill for at least 12 hours.
(13) Churn in your ice cream machine, following manufacturer's instructions.
(14) Store tightly covered in freezer until ready to serve.

INGREDIENTS

1/2 cup of blanched almonds
2 cups of whole milk
1 cup of heavy cream
6 egg yolks
2/3 cup of sugar
pinch of salt
1/2 teaspoon of almond extract

MAKES ONE QUART

CRUNCHY OPTION

For a crunchy almond ice cream, toast and roughly chop an additional 1/2 cup of almonds, let cool and add to the ice cream just before it's finished churning.

APPLE SAUCE ICE CREAM

NOTE: This tastes like apple pie and ice cream rolled into one. Sugar cookies are a good stand-in for the pie crust.

(1) Peel, core and slice apples and put them in a saucepan with the lemon juice, spices, and sugar.
(2) Cook over very low heat, stirring until the apples are soft and richly caramelized. Remove from heat and let cool.
(3) Then purée in blender or food processor. Measure.
(4) Set aside 1/2 cup of the apple sauce for the ice cream (if there's more the cook gets to eat it).
(5) Pour heavy cream into a saucepan with raisins and bring to boiling point. Remove from heat, cover and let steep for 15 or 20 minutes.
(6) Stir apple sauce into cream mixture. When it's all blended, stir in the vanilla.
(7) Pour into a clean bowl and cover with plastic wrap pressed against the surface to prevent a skin forming on top.

INGREDIENTS

2 tart apples
1 tablespoon of freshly squeezed lemon juice
1 teaspoon of cinnamon
1/4 teaspoon of ground cloves
1/2 teaspoon of nutmeg preferably freshly grated
1/2 cup of sugar
3 cups of heavy cream
1/3 cup of raisins
1 teaspoon of vanilla

(8) Chill 12 hours or overnight.
(9) Churn in your ice cream maker, following manufacturer's instructions.
(10) Store tightly covered in freezer until ready to serve.

MAKES ONE QUART

BANANA DAIQUIRI ICE CREAM

NOTE: If you like drinking banana daiquiris, you'll love eating one. This is nice served garnished with slivers of lime.

(1) Purée the bananas in a food processor or blender and measure to make sure you have one cup.
(2) Blend puréed bananas with the lime juice.
(3) Heat the cream in a saucepan and stir in the sugar. Cook, stirring, until the sugar is disolved.
(4) Remove from heat and let cool.
(5) Stir in the banana mixture. Cover with plastic wrap pressed against the surface to prevent a skin forming on top.
(6) Chill for at least 12 hours.
(7) Churn in your ice cream maker, following manufacturer's instructions. When it's almost done add the rum.
(8) Store tightly covered in freezer until ready to serve.

INGREDIENTS

2 very ripe bananas (enough to make 1 cup of purée)
1/4 cup of fresh lime juice
2 cups of heavy cream
1/2 cup of sugar
2 tablespoons of rum

MAKES ONE QUART

CARAMEL ICE CREAM

NOTE: Lush, rich and bittersweet, this is everything ice cream should be. When it's topped with Chocolate Sauce (see page 94) it's even better.

(1) Heat cream to simmering point. You can do this conveniently in a microwave-safe measuring cup with a pouring spout. Set aside.

(2) Put sugar and water in a heavy-bottomed saucepan over medium heat and cook, swirling the mixture around, until it turns a gorgeous amber color. Be very careful - boiling sugar can cause dangerous burns.

(3) When it's beautifully colored, take it off the heat and pour a small amount of the hot cream into the caramel carefully. Stand back because the cream and sugar will bubble up, possibly violently.

(4) When the bubbling subsides pour in the rest of the cream.

(5) Pour it into a bowl and add the salt and vanilla.

INGREDIENTS

3 cups of heavy cream
3/4 cup of sugar
1/4 cup of water
1/4 teaspoon of salt
2 teaspoons of vanilla

(6) Cover with plastic wrap pressed against the surface to prevent a skin forming on top. Chill for at least 12 hours.

(7) Churn in your ice cream maker, following manufacturer's instructions.

(8) Store tightly covered in freezer until ready to serve.

MAKES ONE QUART

CARDAMOM ORANGE
ICE CREAM

NOTE: This has a subtle flavor that people love, even though few guess what it is.

(1) Combine milk and cream in a saucepan over low heat.
(2) Remove cardamom pod shells and discard. Crush the seeds and stir them into the milk and cream.
(3) Add the orange peel and bring to the point of boiling. Take off the heat, cover and set aside to steep for 15 to 20 minutes.
(4) Half fill a large bowl or saucepan with ice or ice water and set aside.
(5) Combine the egg yolks and sugar in another saucepan and whisk until thick and pale.
(6) Strain the cream mixture and stir a little into the egg mixture. Then gradually stir in the rest until it's all combined.
(7) Place pan over low heat and cook, stirring gently, until it thickens enough to coat a spoon. Don't let come to a boil.
(8) Pour into a clean bowl, taste, and add orange extract if you think it needs the flavor.
(9) Then set the bowl in the one containing the ice. Be careful not to let any ice or water get in the ice cream mixture. Stir occasionally until it has cooled.
(10) Cover with plastic wrap pressed against the surface to prevent a skin forming. Chill for at least 12 hours.
(11) Churn in your ice cream machine, following manufacturer's instructions.
(12) Store tightly covered in freezer until ready to serve.

INGREDIENTS

1 1/2 cups of heavy cream
1 1/2 cups of whole milk
6 cardamom pods
2 or 3 inch strip of orange peel
6 egg yolks
1/2 cup of sugar
1/2 teaspoon of orange extract

MAKES ONE QUART

CHERRIES JUBILEE

NOTE: Sophisticated and not too sweet, this is ice cream for grown-ups. Adding chocolate will remind you of the taste of chocolate-covered cherries.

(1) Chop the cherries and combine them with the milk and cream in a saucepan over medium heat.
(2) Cook until the mixture begins to come to a boil, take off heat, cover and let steep for 15 to 20 minutes.
(3) Half fill a large bowl or saucepan with ice or ice water and set aside.
(4) Combine the egg yolks and sugar in another saucepan and whisk until thick and pale.
(5) Stir a little of the steeped cream mixture into the egg mixture. Then gradually stir in the rest until it's all combined.
(6) Place pan over low heat and cook, stirring gently, until it thickens enough to coat a spoon. Don't let it come to a boil.
(7) Pour into a clean bowl, then set the bowl in the one containing the ice. Be careful not to let any ice or water get into the ice cream mixture.

INGREDIENTS

2/3 cup of dried tart cherries (unsweetened)
1 1/2 cups of whole milk
1 1/2 cups of heavy cream
6 egg yolks
1/2 cup of sugar
2 tablespoons of Kirsch

(8) Stir occasionally until it has cooled down. Stir in Kirsch.
(9) Cover with plastic wrap pressed against the surface to prevent a skin forming. Chill for at least 12 hours.
(10) Churn in your ice cream maker, following manufacturer's instructions.
(11) Store tightly covered in freezer until ready to serve.

MAKES ONE QUART

CHOCOLATE OPTION

1/3 cup of finely chopped bitter-sweet or semi-sweet chocolate.

When the ice cream is nearly done churning, mix in the chocolate.

CHESTNUT RUM RAISIN
ICE CREAM

NOTE: To me, this elegant ice cream tastes like a crisp, sunny day in autumn.

(1) Combine raisins and 2 cups of cream in a saucepan and cook over medium heat until it's about to boil. Remove from heat, cover and let steep.

(2) Meanwhile, combine chestnuts and 1 cup of the cream in another saucepan and cook over medium heat until chestnuts are soft, about 10 minutes.

(3) Purée the cream and chestnut mixture in a food processor or blender.

(4) When smooth, stir into cream and raisin mixture.

(5) Stir in sugar and cook over low heat, continuing to stir until sugar is copletely dissolved.

(6) Remove from heat, and mix in the vanilla, salt and rum.

(7) Cover with plastic wrap pressed against the surface to prevent a skin forming. Chill for at least 12 hours.

(8) Churn in your ice cream maker, following manufacturer's instructions.

(9) Store tightly covered in freezer until ready to serve.

INGREDIENTS

1/3 cup of golden raisins
1 cup of cooked, unsweetened chestnuts (I use roasted, whole chestnuts from a jar.)
3 cups of heavy cream
2/3 cup of sugar
1 teaspoon of vanilla
pinch of salt
1/4 cup of rum

MAKES ONE QUART

CHOCOLATE SPICE CREAM

NOTE: This easy to make chocolate ice cream is sweetly spicy. The recipe comes from Roz Cummins, a Boston area food writer.

(1) Melt the chocolate gently in the milk in a double boiler over a medium simmer.
(2) When the chocolate has melted, take it off the heat.
(3) Blend cloves, allspice and cinnamon into sugar.
(4) Stir into milk and chocolate mixture until the sugar is dissolved and the mixture cools.
(5) Add salt and vanilla. Stir this mixture into the two cups of cream.
(6) Cover with plastic wrap pressed against the surface to prevent a skin forming on top.
(7) Chill for at least 12 hours.
(8) Churn in your ice cream maker, following manufacturer's instructions.
(9) Store tightly covered in freezer until ready to serve.

INGREDIENTS

6 ounces of bittersweet chocolate
1 cup of whole milk
1/2 cup of sugar
1/2 teaspoon of cloves
1/2 teaspoon of allspice
1/2 teaspoon of cinnamon
pinch of salt
1 teaspoon of vanilla
2 cups of heavy cream

MAKES ONE QUART

CHOCOLATE HAZELNUT

NOTE: In Italy, the combination of chocolate and hazelnuts is called giandiuja. *It's also called* molto buono.

(1) Spread hazelnuts on a shallow pan and toast in a regular toaster or oven. Let them cool a little, then rub them together in a towel to remove most of the skins. Don't worry if they don't all come off.

(2) Finely grind 1/3 cup of the nuts with a little of the sugar in a food processor

(3) Roughly chop the other 2/3 cup of the hazelnuts and set aside.

(4) Combine milk and cream in a saucepan over low heat.

(5) Add chocolate and stir until it's melted.

(6) Stir in the finely ground hazelnuts.

(7) When the mixture is at the point of boiling, remove from heat, cover and let it steep for 15 or 20 minutes.

(8) Half fill a large bowl or saucepan with ice or ice water and set aside.

(9) In another saucepan, whisk the egg yolks and remaining sugar until thick and pale.

(10) Strain the cream mixture, pressing down on the strainer to get as much of the chocolate cream as possible.

(11) Stir a small amount of the chocolate cream into the eggs, then gradually stir in the rest.

(12) When it's all incorporated, place pan over low heat and cook, stirring gently, until it thickens enough to coat a spoon. Don't let it come to a boil.

(13) Pour into a clean bowl and set that bowl in the one containing the ice. Be careful not to let any ice or water get in the ice cream mixture. Stir occasionally until it has cooled.

(14) Add vanilla extract.

(15) Cover with plastic wrap pressed against the surface to prevent a skin forming on top.

(16) Chill for at least 12 hours.

(17) Churn in your ice creammaker, following manufacturer's instructions.
(18) When it's nearly ready, drop in the reserved, chopped hazelnuts.
(19) Store tightly covered in freezer until ready to serve.

▨ INGREDIENTS

1 cup of hazelnuts
1 1/4 cups of whole milk
1 1/4 cupsof heavy cream
6 ounces of bittersweet or semi-sweet chocolate
1/2 cup of sugar
4 egg yolks
1/2 teaspoon of vanilla

MAKES ONE QUART

CINNAMON BLUEBERRY SWIRL
ICE CREAM

NOTE: This combination looks as good as it tastes. Without the blueberries, it's a wonderful spicy cinnamon ice cream.

(1) Combine milk, cream, vanilla and cinnamon stick in a saucepan and heat to the boiling point. Remove from heat, cover and set aside.

(2) Half fill a large bowl or saucepan with ice or ice water and set aside.

(3) In another saucepan, whisk together the egg yolks with the sugar until they are thick and pale.

(4) Remove the cinnamon stick from the milk mixture and drizzle some of it into the egg mixture.

(5) Gradually stir in the rest. When it is all combined put the pan over medium heat and cook, stirring gently, until it thickens enough to coat the spoon. Do not let it boil.

(6) Pour the mixture into a clean bowl, then set that bowl in the one containing the ice. Be careful not to let any ice or water get into the ice cream mixture. Stir occasionally as it cools.

(7) Cover with plastic wrap pressed against the surface to prevent a skin forming.

(8) Chill for at least 8 hours

(9) Meanwhile purée blueberries with sugar in a food processor or blender. Set aside.

(10) Churn the ice cream mixture in your machine, following manufacturer's instructions.

(11) When the ice cream is done churning, put a third in a container, add a few dollops of blueberry purée and swirl slightly into the ice cream.

(12) Repeat by thirds with the rest of the ice cream and the purée. Don't mix too much or you'll lose the look of the swirl.
(13) Store tightly covered in freezer until ready to serve.
(14) Let it soften a little before serving.

INGREDIENTS

1 1/2 cups of whole milk
1 1/2 cups of heavy cream
1 teaspoon of vanilla
1 small cinnamon stick
6 egg yolks
2/3 cup of sugar
1/2 pint of blueberries
1/8 cup of sugar

MAKES ONE QUART

COCONUT CHOCOLATE CHIP

NOTE: Chewy, white coconut and lush, dark chocolate - this tastes like a favorite candy.

Preheat the oven to 350° F.

(1) Spread coconut on a foil or parchment-lined baking sheet and toast until it barely starts to color, just 3 or 4 minutes. If the coconut pieces are large, chop them. Set aside.
(2) Half fill a large bowl or saucepan with ice or ice water and set aside.
(3) Heat coconut milk in saucepan until barely simmering.
(4) In a separate saucepan, off the heat, whisk sugar, egg yolks and salt until the mixture is thick and pale.
(5) Add hot coconut milk very gradually.
(6) When it's all incorporated, cook the mixture over low heat, stirring constantly, until it thickens enough to coat the spoon. Do not let it boil.
(7) Pour the coconut milk custard into a clean bowl, then set that bowl in the one containing the ice. Be careful not to let any ice or water get into the ice cream mixture.
(8) Stir in vanilla, heavy cream and toasted coconut.
(9) Cover with plastic wrap pressed against surface to prevent a skin forming on top.
(10) Chill for at least 12 hours.
(11) Churn in your ice cream maker, following manufacturer's instructions.
(13) When it's almost ready, mix in the finely chopped chocolate.
(14) Store tightly covered in freezer until ready to serve.

🞖 INGREDIENTS

1/2 cup of unsweetened coconut chips
1 14-ounce can of coconut milk
1/2 cup of sugar
4 egg yolks
pinch of salt
1 teaspoon of vanilla
1 cup of heavy cream
1/3 cup of bittersweet or semi-sweet chocolate, finely chopped

MAKES ONE QUART

COFFEE WITH CHOCOLATE-COVERED ESPRESSO BEANS

NOTE: Bittersweet, creamy and crunchy, this ice cream gives you a double dose of coffee and chocolate too.

(1) Combine milk and cream in saucepan and warm over low heat.
(2) Add the ground coffee, stir and heat until it's about to simmer.
(3) Shut off heat, cover and let the mixture steep for half an hour or so. Give it a stir from time to time.
(4) Half fill a large bowl or saucepan with ice or ice water and set aside.
(5) In another saucepan, whisk egg yolks and sugar until thick and pale.
(6) Strain the coffee mixture carefully to get rid of the coffee grounds, then rewarm it.
(7) Stir it gradually into the egg mixture.
(8) When it's all incorporated, cook over low heat, stirring constantly, until it thickens enough to coat the spoon. Do not let it boil.
(9) Place the pan of coffee custard in the bowl with the ice water and continue to stir until it cools.
(10) Cover with plastic wrap pressed against the surface to prevent a skin forming on top.
(11) Chill for at least 12 hours.

INGREDIENTS

2 cups of whole milk
1 cup of heavy cream
1/3 cup of finely ground espresso or dark roast coffee
5 egg yolks
1/2 cup of sugar
1/2 cup of chocolate-covered espresso beans

(12) Put the coffee beans in a zip lock bag and smack with a rolling pin or heavy bottle until they're chopped up. Set aside.
(13) Churn the ice cream mixture in your machine, following manufacturer's instructions.
(14) When it's almost ready, mix in the chopped chocolate-covered coffee beans.
(15) Store tightly covered in your freezer until ready to serve.

MAKES ONE QUART

CRANBERRY-PISTACHIO
ICE CREAM

NOTE: Festive red and green colors make this perfect for the holiday season, but it's more than pretty. The combination of tart berries and rich pistachios is wonderful.

(1) Chop the cranberries and combine them with the milk and cream in a saucepan over medium heat.
(2) Cook until the mixture begins to come to a boil, take off the heat, cover and let steep for 15 to 20 minutes.
(3) Half fill a large bowl or saucepan with ice or ice water and set aside.
(4) Combine the egg yolks and sugar in another saucepan and whisk until thick and pale. Stir a little of the steeped cream mixture into the egg mixture. Then gradually stir in the rest until it's all combined.
(5) Place pan over low heat and cook, stirring gently, until it thickens enough to coat a spoon. Don't let it come to a boil.
(6) Pour into a clean bowl, then set that bowl in the one containing the ice. Be careful not to let any ice or water get in the ice cream mixture.
(7) Stir occasionally until it has cooled. Stir in salt and vanilla and almond extract.
(8) Cover with plastic wrap pressed against the surface to prevent a skin forming.

INGREDIENTS

1/3 cup of dried cranberries
2 cups of whole milk
1 cup of cream
6 egg yolks
1/2 cup of sugar
pinch of salt
1/2 teaspoon of vanilla extract
1/4 teaspoon of almond extract
1/3 cup of chopped, toasted pistachios

(9) Chill for at least 12 hours.
(10) Churn the ice cream mixture in your machine, following manufacturer's instructions.
(11) When it's almost ready, mix in the chopped, toasted pistachios.
(12) Store tightly covered in freezer until ready to serve.

MAKES ONE QUART

CREME DE PROVENCE

NOTE: In Provence, the air is fragrant with the scent of lavender. When you make this ice cream, close your eyes and breathe deeply as you stir the lavender into the milk, and you can pretend you're there.

(1) Combine milk, lavender and orange peel in saucepan over medium heat. Bring to a simmer and then take it off the heat and let it infuse for 15 minutes.

(2) Half fill a large bowl or saucepan with ice or ice water and set aside.

(3) In another saucepan, combine the egg yolks, sugar and honey and whisk until the mixture thickens and becomes pale.

(4) Strain the milk mixture and gradually stir it into the egg mixture.

(5) When it's all incorporated, return the pan to the heat and cook, stirring gently, until it thickens enough to coat the spoon. Do not let it boil.

(6) Pour into a clean bowl and set in the bowl containing the ice. Be careful not to let any ice or water get in the ice cream mixture.

(7) Mix in the heavy cream and orange extract. Stir occasionally until it's cool.

INGREDIENTS

1 1/2 cups of whole milk
2 tablespoons of dried lavender
2 or 3 inch strip of orange peel
6 egg yolks
1/4 cup of sugar
1/4 cup of honey
1 1/2 cups of heavy cream
1/2 teaspoon of orange extract

(8) Cover with plastic wrap pressed against the surface to prevent a skin forming. Chill for at least 12 hours.

(9) Churn mixture in your ice cream machine, following manufacturer's instructions.

(10) Store tightly covered in freezer until ready to serve.

MAKES ONE QUART

EARL GREY'S ICE CREAM

NOTE: Tea and cookies taste even better when the tea is ice cream. Use Earl Grey tea or your favorite flavor.

(1) Pour milk into saucepan and bring to the boiling point.
(2) Stir in tea, remove from heat, cover and let steep for five minutes. Strain.
(3) Half fill a large bowl or saucepan with ice or ice water and set aside.
(4) Combine the egg yolks and sugar in another saucepan and whisk until thick and pale.
(5) Stir a little of the steeped milk mixture into the egg mixture. Then gradually stir in the rest until it's all combined.
(6) Place pan over low heat and cook, stirring gently until it thickens enough to coat a spoon. Don't let it come to a boil.
(7) Pour into a clean bowl, then set that bowl in the one containing the ice. Be careful not to let any ice or water get in the ice cream mixture.
(8) Mix in the cream and stir occasionally until it has cooled.

INGREDIENTS

2 cups of whole milk
1 tablespoon of Earl Grey tea
6 egg yolks
1/2 cup of sugar
1 cup of heavy cream

---

(9) Cover with plastic wrap pressed against the surface to prevent a skin forming.
(10) Chill for at least 12 hours or overnight.
(11) Churn the ice cream mixture in your machine, following manufacturer's instructions.
(12) Store tightly covered in freezer until ready to serve.

MAKES ONE QUART

FIVE-SPICE CREAM

NOTE: Spicy nuts give this ice cream pizzazz. By themselves, the nuts are a great snack or topping for other ice creams.

(1) Toss butter, nuts, five-spice powder and salt together in a bowl. Pour onto a parchment lined cookie sheet and bake, stirring occasionally, at 375º F. for 10 minutes. Set aside.

(2) Combine milk and cream in a saucepan over low heat, and bring to the point of boiling. Take off the heat.

(3) Half fill a large bowl or saucepan with ice or ice water and set aside.

(4) Combine the egg yolks and sugar in another saucepan and whisk until thick and pale.

(5) Stir a little of the cream into the egg mixture. Then gradually stir in the rest until it's all combined.

(6) Place pan over a low heat and cook, stirring gently, until it thickens enough to coat a spoon. Don't let it come to a boil.

(7) Pour into a clean bowl, then set that bowl in the one containing the ice. Be careful not to let any ice or water get into the cream mixture.

(8) Stir occasionally until it has cooled. Stir in vanilla.

(9) Cover with plastic wrap pressed against the surface to prevent a skin forming on top.

(10) Chill for at least 12 hours or overnight.

(11) Churn in your ice cream maker, following manufacturer's instructions.

(12) Just before it's done, stir in the chopped spiced nuts.

(13) Store tightly covered in freezer until ready to serve.

MAKES ONE QUART

🪷 INGREDIENTS

FIRST (Step 1)
2 tablespoons of melted butter
1 cup of roughly chopped, mixed
   nuts (walnuts, pecans, hazelnuts)
2 tablespoons of five-spice powder
pinch of salt

NEXT (Steps 2-8)
1 1/2 cups of whole milk
1 1/2 cups of heavy cream
6 egg yolks
1/2 cup of sugar
1 teaspoon of vanilla extract

GINGER - GINGER ICE CREAM

NOTE: The combination of fresh ginger and candied ginger gives this ice cream a sweet heat as well as a bit of crunch.

(1) Heat milk and cream to simmer point, remove from heat and add fresh ginger. Set aside and let steep for at least 15 minutes.
(2) Half fill a bowl with ice or ice water and set aside.
(3) In a saucepan, whisk together the egg yolks and sugar until thick and pale. Drizzle in a little of the milk mixture and continue mixing.
(4) Continue slowly adding milk mixture to egg and sugar mixture. When they are all combined, put the pan over medium heat and cook, stirring constantly, until the mixture thickens and coats a spoon. Do not let it boil.
(5) Strain the mixture into a bowl and place the bowl in the one containing the ice. Be careful not to let any ice or water get into the ice cream mixture.
(6) Add salt and vanilla. Stir occasionally.
(7) When it's cool, cover with plastic wrap pressed against the surface to prevent skin forming on top.
(8) Chill for at least 12 hours or overnight.
(9) Churn in your ice cream maker, following manufacturer's instructions.
(10) Just before it's done, stir in the candied ginger.
(11) Store tightly covered in freezer until ready to serve.

MAKES ONE QUART

🎀 INGREDIENTS

1 1/2 cups of whole milk
1 1/2 cups of heavy cream
4 tablespoons of peeled, roughly chopped, fresh ginger
6 egg yolks
2/3 cup of sugar
pinch of salt
1 teaspoon of vanilla
1/4 cup of chopped, candied ginger

NUTTY OPTION

In addition to the candied ginger, add 2 or 3 tablespoons of toasted walnut pieces.

LEMON ICE CREAM

NOTE: Sweet cream and puckery lemon - opposites attract and make a perfect match in this tart ice cream.

(1) Slice peel from one lemon, avoiding white pith. Grate enough of the peel to make one tablespoon and set aside. Leave the rest in slices and set aside.

(2) Squeeze enough of the lemons to make 1/3 cup of juice.

(3) Combine cream and milk in a saucepan over medium heat. Stir in the sliced lemon peel and bring the mixture slowly to boiling point, then take off heat and let the flavor of the peel infuse for 15-20 minutes.

(4) Half fill a large bowl with ice or ice water. Set aside.

(5) In another saucepan, whisk together the egg yolks and sugar until thick and pale.

(6) Add the milk mixture to the egg mixture slowly until it is all incorporated. Then return to heat and cook, stirring constantly, until it thickens enough to coat a spoon. Do not let it boil.

(7) Strain into a bowl and set in the bowl with ice. Then stir up to 1/3 cup of freshly squeezed lemon juice and the lemon extract, according to your taste.

(8) When it's cool, cover with plastic wrap pressed against surface to prevent a skin forming on top.

(9) Chill for at least 12 hours.

(10) Churn in your ice cream maker, following manufacturer's instructions.

(11) Just before it's done, stir in the reserved, finely grated peel. Store tightly covered in freezer until ready to serve.

MAKES ONE QUART

◩ INGREDIENTS

2-3 lemons
1 1/2 cups of heavy cream
1 1/2 cups of whole milk
6 egg yolks
3/4 cup of sugar
1/2 teaspoon of lemon extract

MOCHA ICE CREAM

NOTE: The Oxford Companion to Food defines "mocha" as the name given to coffee produced in the Yemeni port of Moka. Later, it became associated with the flavor of coffee when combined with chocolate. They make a great pair.

(1) Combine coffee beans, milk and cream in a saucepan and bring almost to boiling point. Remove from heat, cover and let steep for 15 to 20 minutes.

(2) In another saucepan, whisk the egg yolks and sugar until thick and pale. Whisk in cocoa.

(3) Half fill a large bowl or saucepan with ice or ice water and set aside.

(4) Strain the coffee beans out of the cream mixture.

(5) Stir a small amount of the cream into the egg, sugar and cocoa mixture, then gradually stir in the rest.

(6) When it's all incorporated, place pan over low heat and cook, stirring gently, until it thickens enough to coat a spoon. Don't let it come to a boil.

(7) Pour into a clean bowl. Set that bowl in the one containing the ice. Be careful not to let any ice or water get in the ice cream mixture.

(8) Stir occasionally until it has cooled. Stir in salt and vanilla extract.

(9) Cover with plastic wrap pressed against the surface to prevent a skin forming on top.

(10) Chill for at least 12 hours or overnight.

(11) Churn in your ice cream maker, following manufacturer's instructions.

(12) Store tightly covered in freezer until ready to serve.

▨ INGREDIENTS

1/3 cup of your favorite coffee beans
2 cups of whole milk
1 cup of heavy cream
4 egg yolks
2/3 cup of sugar
1/3 cup of unsweetened Dutch process cocoa
pinch of salt
1/2 teaspoon of vanilla

MAKES ONE QUART

NUTTY OPTION

1/2 cup of toasted chopped walnuts

Note: Add the toasted walnuts when the ice cream is nearly done churning.

OLOROSO ICE CREAM

NOTE: The nutty flavor of sherry is terrific in ice cream, especially when paired with raisins and pine nuts.

(1) Combine the milk, cream, orange and lemon peels and raisins in a saucepan and bring to the point of boiling. Take off the heat, cover and let steep for 15-20 minutes. Pick out peels.
(2) Half fill a large bowl or saucepan with ice or ice water; set aside.
(3) Combine the egg yolks and sugar in another saucepan and whisk until thick and pale.
(4) Whisk in the sherry.
(5) Stir a little of the steeped cream mixture into the egg mixture. Then gradually stir in the rest until it's all combined.
(6) Cook the mixture over low heat, stirring gently until it thickens enough to coat a spoon. Don't let it come to a boil.
(7) Pour into a clean bowl and set in the bowl containing the ice. Be careful not to let any ice or water get in the ice cream mixture.
(8) Stir occasionally until it has cooled. Cover with plastic wrap pressed against the surface to prevent a skin forming on top.

▪ INGREDIENTS

1 1/2 cups of whole milk
1 1/2 cups of heavy cream
2-inch strip of orange peel
2-inch strip of lemon peel
1/3 cup of raisins or currants
5 egg yolks
1/2 cup of sugar
1/4 cup of sherry - Oloroso or Amontillado
1/4 cup of toasted pine nuts

(9) Chill for at least 12 hours or overnight.
(10) Toast pine nuts and set aside.
(11) Churn ice cream mixture in your ice cream maker, following manufacturer's instructions.
(12) Just before it's done, add pine nuts, making sure they're mixed well throughout.
(13) Store tightly covered in freezer until ready to serve.

MAKES ONE QUART

ORANGE FLOWER WATER ICE CREAM

NOTE: In the 18th century, orange flower water was as popular as vanilla is today. Its fragrant aroma and delicate flavor are still popular in Middle Eastern cuisines, and Middle Eastern neighborhood markets are good places to find it. If you've never tasted it, you're in for a delightful new experience.

(1) Combine milk and cream in a saucepan over low heat and bring to the simmer point.

(2) Half fill a large bowl or saucepan with ice or ice water and set aside.

(3) In another pan, whisk the egg yolks and sugar until thick and pale. Gradually stir the cream into the egg yolk mixture.

(4) When it is all incorporated, return the pan to the heat and cook, stirring constantly, until it thickens enough to coat the spoon. Do not let it boil.

(5) Pour it into a clean bowl and set it in the bowl of ice. Be careful not to let any ice or water get in the ice cream mixture.

(6) Stir in the orange flower water, and continue to stir occasionally until it's cool.

(7) Cover with plastic wrap pressed against the surface to prevent a skin forming on top.

❖ INGREDIENTS

1 1/2 cups of whole milk
1 1/2 cups of heavy cream
6 egg yolks
2/3 cups of sugar
1 1/2 teasoons of orange flower water

(8) Chill for at least 12 hours or overnight.

(9) Churn mixture in your ice cream maker, following manufacturer's instructions.

(10) Store tightly covered in freezer until ready to serve.

MAKES ONE QUART

ORANGE MARMALADE ICE CREAM

NOTE: Cooks used to substitute marmalade or jam when fresh fruits were out of season. I use it because the bracing bittersweet flavor of the marmalade pairs so well with the lushness of the cream.

(1) If the marmalade has very long pieces of peel, chop it a little so the pieces are roughly a half-inch long.
(2) Mix marmalade, lemon juice and cream together in a bowl and chill for at least 12 hours or overnight.
(3) Churn in your ice cream maker, following manufacturer's instructions.
(4) When it is nearly done add the liqueur.
(5) Store tightly covered in freezer until ready to serve.

INGREDIENTS

1 cup of top-quality Seville orange marmalade
1 teaspoon of freshly squeezed lemon juice
3 cups of heavy cream
2 tablespoons of orange liqueur, such as Grand Marnier

MAKES ONE QUART

PINA COLADA ICE CREAM

NOTE: This summery ice cream is the perfect finale to a dinner with a little heat in it, like chili or a spicy curry. Try serving it with toasted coconut sprinkled on top.

(1) Heat coconut milk in a medium saucepan until it's ready to simmer.
(2) Half fill a large bowl or saucepan with ice or ice water and set aside.
(3) In another saucepan, whisk egg yolks and sugar until thick and pale.
(4) Gradually stir coconut milk into egg mixture. Cook stirring gently, over low heat until the mixture thickens enough to coat a spoon. Don't let it boil.
(5) Pour into a clean bowl and set it in the bowl with the ice. Be careful not to let any ice or water get in the ice cream mixture.
(6) Stir in the heavy cream, pineapple, and salt.
(7) Cover with plastic wrap pressed against the surface to prevent a skin forming on top.
(8) Chill for at least 12 hours.

INGREDIENTS

14-ounce can of coconut milk (1 3/4 cups)
4 egg yolks
1/2 cup of sugar
1 1/4 cups of heavy cream
1/2 cup of crushed pineapple (canned in its own juice, not in syrup, and drained)
pinch of salt
3 tablespoons of dark rum

(9) Churn the mixture in your ice cream maker, following manufacturer's instructions.
(10) Blend in the rum just before it's done.
(11) Store tightly covered in freezer until ready to serve.

MAKES ONE QUART

PISTACHIO ICE CREAM

NOTE: Pistachio is one of the world's great ice cream flavors. Cooking the nuts in the milk, and then straining them out, gives your mixture maximum pistachio flavor. Adding toasted pistachios at the end gives it crunch and even more flavor.

(1) Toast all of the pistachios. Set 2/3 cup aside. Roughly chop the remaining 1/3 cup.

(2) Combine milk and the 1/3 cup of roughly chopped pistachios in a medium saucepan and heat until the milk is about to come to the boil. Remove from heat, cover and let steep for 15 to 20 minutes.

(3) Half fill a large bowl or saucepan with ice or ice water and set aside.

(4) In another saucepan, combine the egg yolks and sugar and whisk until thick and pale.

(5) Strain the pistachio and milk mixture and discard the nuts. Then pour the milk slowly into the egg and sugar mixture.

(6) Cook over low heat stirring constantly until it thickens enough to coat a spoon. Don't let it come to a boil.

(7) Remove from heat and set the pan in the bowl containing the ice. Be careful not to let any ice or water get in the ice cream mixture.

INGREDIENTS

1 cup of pistachio nuts
1 1/2 cups of whole milk
6 egg yolks
2/3 cup of sugar
1 1/2 cups of heavy cream
pinch of salt
1/2 teaspoon of almond extract

(8) Stir in the cream, salt and almond extract; continue stirring occasionally until the mixture cools.

(9) Then cover with clear plastic wrap pressed against the surface to prevent a skin forming on top.

(10) Chill for at least 12 hours or overnight.

(11) Roughly chop the reserved pistachios. Churn ice cream mixture in your ice cream maker, following manufacturer's instructions. Just before it's done add the pistachios.

(12) Store tightly covered in freezer until ready to serve.

MAKES ONE QUART

PUMPKIN PRALINE

NOTE: This is perfect for Thanksgiving, but too good to have just once a year. The caramelized pecans are good on their own or sprinkled over ice creams.

(1) Toast the pecans and sprinkle with a pinch of salt. Put sugar and water in a heavy-bottomed saucepan over medium heat and cook, swirling the mixture around, until it turns a gorgeous amber color. Be very careful - boiling sugar can cause dangerous burns. When it's lightly colored, remove from heat and add the pecans. Working quickly, pour the mixture onto a buttered cookie sheet. Let cool, then break up into small pieces with a knife.

(2) Combine pumpkin purée and cream in a saucepan over medium heat and stir until thoroughly mixed.

(3) Combine sugars with spices, then stir into pumpkin mixture. Simmer, stirring until sugars dissolve.

(4) Remove from heat, add salt and vanilla and let cool, then cover with plastic wrap and refrigerate until well chilled, preferably overnight.

(5) Churn in your ice cream maker, following manufacturer's instructions. When it's nearly done, mix in the finely chopped praline.

(6) Store tightly covered in freezer until ready to serve.

INGREDIENTS

FIRST (Step 1)

1 cup of sugar
1/2 cup of water
1 cup of pecans
pinch of salt

NEXT (Steps 2 - 6)

1 cup of unsweetened pumpkin purée
3 cups of heavy cream
2/3 cup of white sugar
1/3 cup of brown sugar
1/4 teaspoon of ground cloves
1/2 teaspoon of ground ginger
1/2 teaspoon of freshly ground nutmeg
1 teaspoon of ground cinnamon
pinch of salt
1 teaspoon of vanilla extract

MAKES ONE QUART

RASPBERRY ICE CREAM

NOTE: Fresh is best, but even with frozen raspberries this is a lovely, flavorful ice cream. It's especially delectable paired with almond ice cream and meringues.

(1) Purée the raspberries in a food processor or blender.
(2) Combine sugar and cream in a saucepan, stir in raspberry purée and cook over medium heat until it comes to a simmer.
(3) Add lemon juice and stir thoroughly.
(4) Take off heat, strain into a bowl, and cover with plastic wrap pressed against the surface to prevent a skin forming on top.
(5) Chill for at least 12 hours.
(6) Churn in your ice cream maker, following manufacturer's instructions.
(7) Store tightly covered in freezer until ready to serve.

▨ INGREDIENTS

2 cups (one pint) of fresh or unsweetened frozen raspberries
1/2 cup of sugar
2 1/2 cups of heavy cream
1 teaspoon of freshly squeezed lemon juice

MAKES ONE QUART

ROYAL ICE CREAM

NOTE: I adapted this from a recipe of the same name by Mr Borella, confectioner to the Spanish Ambassador in England in the late 18th century. The bright, clean flavor of the coriander is lovely with the candied peel and almonds.

(1) Combine milk, cream, coriander, and lemon peel in a medium-size saucepan and bring nearly to a boil. Remove from heat, cover, and steep for 15 minutes or so.
(2) Half fill a large bowl or saucepan with ice or ice water and set aside.
(3) In another saucepan, combine the egg yolks and sugar and whisk until thick and pale.
(4) Strain the milk mixture and gradually stir it into the egg and sugar mixture. Cook over low heat, stirring constantly, until it thickens enough to coat a spoon. Don't let it come to a boil.
(5) Remove from heat, pour into a clean bowl and set in the bowl containing the ice. Be careful not to let any ice or water get into the ice cream mixture. Stir occasionally until it cools.
(6) Cover with plastic wrap and refrigerate, preferably overnight.
(7) Toast and roughly chop the almonds. Chop the peel finely, as large pieces could freeze to a tooth-crunching consistency. Set both aside.
(8) Churn the chilled mixture in your ice cream maker, following manufacturer's instructions.
(9) While it's mixing add the finely chopped peel and the chopped toasted almonds.
(10) Store tightly covered in freezer until ready to serve.

INGREDIENTS

1 1/2 cups of whole milk
1 1/2 cups of heavy cream
2 teaspoons of ground coriander
1 2-inch strip of lemon peel
6 egg yolks
2/3 cup of sugar
1/3 cup of almonds
1/3 cup candied lemon or citron peel

MAKES ONE QUART

STRAWBERRY-RHUBARB ICE CREAM

NOTE: Strawberries and rhubarb are always paired in pies and muffins, seldom matched in ice cream. But the lushness of cream gives their sweet and tart flavors new depth.

(1) Cook rhubarb and 1 tablespoon of the orange juice in a saucepan until the rhubarb is tender, about 5 minutes. Let cool, then purée in a food processor or blender.

(2) Measure 1 cup, pour into a bowl, and set aside to cool.

(3) Purée strawberries and the second tablespoon of orange juice in a food processor or blender, measure 1 cup and mix with rhubarb.

(4) Meanwhile combine cream, milk and sugar in a saucepan and slowly bring to the point of boiling, stirring to dissolve sugar completely. Let cool, then combine with the fruit mixture.

(5) Cover with plastic wrap pressed against the surface to prevent a skin forming on top.

INGREDIENTS

2 cups of roughly chopped rhubarb
2 tablespoons of orange juice, divided
1 pint of hulled strawberries
1 cup of heavy cream
1/2 cup of whole milk
3/4 cup of sugar (If the strawberries are very sweet, use 2/3 cup sugar)

(6) Chill for at least 12 hours.
(7) Churn in your ice cream maker, following manufacturer's instructions.
(8) Store tightly covered in freezer until ready to serve.

MAKES ONE QUART

VANILLA PLAIN & PERFECT

NOTE: Plain vanilla is perfect as it is. Or you can serve it atop pies or cakes, adorned with sauces, topped with nuts, or mixed with add-ins. It's also nice paired with a more assertive ice cream such as Pumpkin Praline or Orange Marmalade.

(1) Combine milk and cream in a saucepan over low heat. Split the vanilla beans in half lengthwise and scrape their seeds into the milk and cream mixture. Add scraped beans, then bring the mixture just to a boil. Turn off the heat, cover the pan and let the mixture steep for 15 minutes or so.

(2) Half fill a large bowl or saucepan with ice or ice water and set aside.

(3) In another saucepan, whisk the egg yolks and sugar until thick and pale. Remove the scraped beans* from the cream mixture, then slowly stir the cream into the egg yolk mixture. When it's all incorporated, return the pan to the heat and cook, stirring constantly, until it thickens enough to coat a spoon. Do not let it boil.

(4) Pour into a clean bowl and set it in the bowl of ice. Be careful not to let any ice or water get into the ice cream mixture. Stir occasionally until it's cool.

(5) Cover with plastic wrap pressed down to prevent a skin forming on top.

(6) Chill for at least 12 hours or overnight.

(7) Churn in your ice cream maker, following manufacturer's instructions.

(8) Store tightly covered in freezer until ready to serve.

* The vanilla beans can be rinsed off and dried for re-use. If you dry them in a slow oven, you'll also perfume your kitchen. After they're dry, put them in a small jar of sugar to make vanilla sugar for baking.

INGREDIENTS

1 1/2 cups of whole milk
1 1/2 cups of heavy cream
2 vanilla beans
6 egg yolks
2/3 cup of sugar

MAKES ONE QUART

WHITE COFFEE ICE CREAM

NOTE: A favorite of 18th century cooks like M. Emy, this delectable ice cream has intense coffee aroma and flavor, but it's deceptively pale in color. It's also good topped with Coffee Syrup (see page 95).

(1) Combine coffee beans and milk in a medium-size saucepan over low heat and cook until about to boil. Remove from heat, cover and let steep for 10 to 15 minutes. Strain.

(2) Half fill a large bowl or saucepan with ice or ice water; set aside.

(3) In another saucepan, whisk the egg yolks and sugar until thick and pale. Gradually stir the strained milk into the egg yolk mixture.

(4) When it's all incorporated, return the pan to the heat and cook, stirring constantly until it thickens enough to coat a spoon. Do not let it boil.

(5) When it's ready, pour into a clean bowl and set that in the one containing the ice. Be careful not to let any ice or water get into the ice cream mixture.

▨ INGREDIENTS

2/3 cup of coffee beans
1 1/2 cups of whole milk
6 egg yolks
1/2 cup of sugar
1 1/2 cups of heavy cream
1 teaspoon of vanilla

(6) Stir in the heavy cream and vanilla and then continue stirring occasionally until it's cooled off.

(7) Cover with plastic wrap pressed against the surface to prevent a skin forming on top.

(8) Chill for at least 12 hours.

(9) Churn in your ice cream maker, following manufacturer's instructions.

(10) Store tightly covered in freezer until ready to serve.

MAKES ONE QUART

FROZEN MOUSSES

NOTE: You don't even need an ice cream maker for these lighter-than-air desserts.

BISCUIT TORTONI

(1) Grind cookies to fine crumbs (but not a powder) in a food processor or blender.
(2) In a medium-sized bowl, whip cream with sugar until cream forms soft peaks.
(3) Carefully fold in crushed cookies (reserving a tablespoon or two for topping) and rum.
(4) In another bowl, beat the egg whites until they form stiff peaks. Gently fold into cream mixture.
(5) Spoon the mixture into paper-lined cupcake tins, swirling the mixture into peaks.
(6) Sprinkle with the reserved cookie crumbs.
(7) Cover with plastic wrap and freeze until firm.

▥ INGREDIENTS

1/2 cup of amaretti cookies
1 cup of heavy cream
1/4 cup of confectioners' sugar
3 tablespoons of rum
2 egg whites

MAKES 12

CHOCOLATE MOUSSE

NOTE: This is light and foamy, but it's rich enough for a true chocolate lover.

(1) Using a hand-held mixer or a whisk, mix egg yolks and sugar in a saucepan over a larger pan of simmering water. (or use a double boiler)

(2) Cook, mixing constantly, until it becomes thick and begins to pale. Don't let it come to a boil.

(3) With a spoon or rubber spatula, stir in chocolate and continue stirring until the chocolate is completely melted.

(4) Remove from heat, pour into a clean bowl and stir in the vanilla. Let Cool. If it gets cold and solidifies, zap it in the microwave for 5 seconds or so.

(5) Beat egg whites until frothy, add salt, and continue to beat until they hold stiff peaks.

(6) In a separate bowl, whip cream and set aside.

(7) Stir a little of the egg white into the chocolate mixture to loosen it. Then, very gently, fold the rest of the egg whites, and then the whipped cream into the chocolate mixture.

(8) Spoon into paper-lined cupcake tins, swirling it into peaks.

(9) Cover and put in freezer until firm.

MAKES 12

🟦 INGREDIENTS

3 egg yolks
1/4 cup of sugar
1/2 cup of semi-sweet chocolate chips (or chopped, semi-sweet chocolate)
1 teaspoon of vanilla
3 egg whites
pinch of salt
1 cup of heavy cream

GRAND OPTION

1 tablespoon Grand Marnier (or other liqueur)

Stir into the chocolate mixture when you add the vanilla for a slight hint of orange.

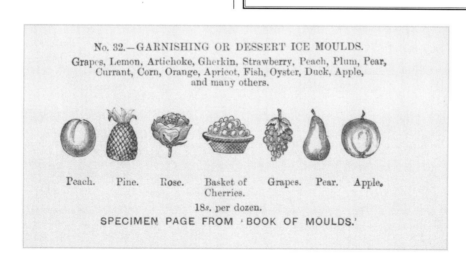

MAPLE PECAN MOUSSE

NOTE: Frothy cream, crunchy pecans and the mellow sweetness of maple make one terrific mousse.

(1) Whisk egg yolks in a saucepan over a larger pan of simmering water. (Or use a double boiler.)
(2) Add maple syrup. Cook, whisking constantly, until it's thick and begins to pale.
(3) Take off heat, pour into a clean bowl and stir in vanilla. Stir occasionally until it cools.
(4) Chill in a refrigerator until cold.
(5) Toast nuts and set aside to cool.
(6) Stir the pecans into the cold maple mixture, mixing thoroughly.
(7) In another bowl, beat the egg whites until they're frothy, add salt, and beat until they form stiff peaks. Set aside.
(8) Whip the cream and set aside.
(9) Using a rubber spatula, very gently fold the whipped cream into the maple-pecan mixture. Fold in the stiffly beaten egg whites, again working carefully to keep the mixture light and fluffy.

INGREDIENTS

4 egg yolks
3/4 cup of genuine maple syrup
1 teaspoon of vanilla
1/2 cup of finely chopped pecans (or walnuts) plus a little extra for topping
2 egg whites
pinch of salt
1 cup of heavy cream

(10) Spoon it into paper-lined cup cake tins, swirling it into peaks. Sprinkle with extra nuts.
(11) Cover with a foil tent, and put in freezer until firm.

MAKES 12

SORBETS

ALMOND SORBET

NOTE: This makes a fragrant, pure-white sorbet. It tastes - and looks - terrific with the Blackberry Sauce on page 91. I use Monin almond syrup, sold as a coffee add-in. Hazelnut syrup would work well too.

(1) Make a simple syrup by heating 1 cup of water and sugar in a saucepan just until the sugar is dissolved. Don't cook it any longer because it will start to caramelize and the flavor will change.
(2) Take off the heat, and stir in the almond syrup, lemon juice, almond extract and the additional water. Mix well and chill, preferably overnight.
(3) Taste, and if you think it's too sweet, add a bit more water.
(4) Churn in your ice cream maker, following manufacturer's instructions.
(5) Store in tightly covered container in your freezer.

INGREDIENTS

3/4 cup of sugar
1 cup of water
1/2 cup of almond syrup
1 tablespoon of lemon juice
1/2 teaspoon of almond extract
1 1/2 cups of water

MAKES A SCANT QUART

CANTALOUPE & PORT SORBET

NOTE: *Cantaloupe and port are such natural flavor partners that a traditional dessert consists of cantaloupe halves scooped out and filled with port. This recipe gives you the same blend of flavors in one wonderful sorbet.*

(1) Cut up the cantaloupe and measure. To make a quart of sorbet, you'll need three cups.
(2) In a blender or food processor, purée cantaloupe with the salt and sugar until the sugar is thoroughly blended throughout the mixture.
(3) Add the port and the orange juice and blend.
(4) Chill the mixture in the refrigerator, preferably overnight.
(5) Then churn in your ice cream maker, following manufacturer's instructions.
(6) Store in tightly covered containers in your freezer.

▣ INGREDIENTS

One large or two small cantaloupes, peeled, seeded and cut up to make 3 cups
Pinch of salt
3/4 cup of sugar
1/4 cup of port
3 tablespoons of orange juice

MAKES ONE QUART

CHOCOLATE SORBET A L'EMY

NOTE: This is my adaptation of Emy's 18th-century ice. The combination of chocolate and cocoa makes it as rich and mouth-filling as an ice cream.

(1) Combine water and sugar in a saucepan over medium heat, stirring until the sugar dissolves.
(2) Add chocolate and cocoa, stir to melt chocolate and blend in cocoa.
(3) Bring the mixture to the point of boiling, but don't let it boil.
(4) Remove from heat and stir in the vanilla, cinnamon, cloves and lemon peel.
(5) Let the flavors infuse, stirring occasionally as the mixture cools. Then strain into a clean bowl.
(6) Cover with plastic wrap, pressed against the surface, and chill for several hours or overnight.
(7) When you're ready to freeze the sorbet, whisk the egg white lightly and set aside.
(8) Pour the sorbet mixture into your ice cream maker and churn, following manufacturer's instructions
(9) When it's nearly done, whisk egg white until it's frothy and mix in.

INGREDIENTS

3 cups of water
1 cup of sugar
4 ounces of bittersweet chocolate, chopped
1/4 cup of unsweetened cocoa powder
1 teaspoon of vanilla
1/2 teaspoon of cinnamon
1/2 teaspoon of ground cloves
1 2-inch strip of lemon peel
1 egg white

(10) Store tightly covered in container in your freezer.

MAKES ONE QUART

CINNAMON ICE *al la* LATINI

NOTE: Back in the 17th century, Latini mixed pine nuts into his cinnamon ice. It's still a good idea. The rich, buttery taste of the pine nuts contrasts with the warmth and spice of cinnamon and cloves. This is wonderful with fall and winter fruits like poached pears or baked apples.

(1) Pour water into a saucepan over medium heat, add sugar and stir to dissolve.
(2) Break the cinnamon sticks in half and add them to the syrup along with the cloves and lemon juice.
(3) Remove from heat and let cool.
(4) Strain into a clean bowl, cover, and chill for several hours or overnight.
(5) When you're ready to freeze the sorbet, toast the pine nuts for about 5 minutes in a low oven. I use a toaster oven set at 250º F. Watch carefully, they burn easily.
(6) When they're lightly browned and fragrant. remove them from the oven and set aside to cool.
(7) Whisk the egg white to a light froth, and set it aside.

▦ INGREDIENTS

3 cups of water
1 1/2 cups of sugar
2 cinnamon sticks, about two inches long.
1/4 teaspoon of ground cloves
2 tablespoons of lemon juice
1 egg white
1/4 cup of pine nuts

(8) Pour sorbet mixture into your ice cream maker, and churn, following manufacturer's instructions.
(9) When it's almost ready, mix in the egg white, then add the pine nuts and mix just enough to blend them throughout.
(10) Store tightly covered in a container in your freezer.

MAKES ONE QUART

FENNEL LEMON SORBET

NOTE: This is a lovely, aromatic sorbet from Elizabeth Riely, author of The Chef's Companion: A Concise Dictionary of Culinary Terms, *John Wiley & Sons.*

(1) Remove the leaves from the fennel and reserve them. Quarter the bulb and cut each quarter in half, slice the bulb and any stalks. Put them in a saucepan with 2 cups water. Bring water to a boil, cover, and simmer until the fennel is tender, about 20 minutes; let the fennel cool in the covered pot.

(2) Purée the fennel in a food processor or food mill, then pass it through a sieve, pressing on the pulp with the back of a spoon to extract the liquid. Discard the pulp. Save the puréed fennel with its cooking water.

(3) Stir the lemon juice and sugar until dissolved. Combine the lemon and fennel liquids, cover and chill thoroughly.

(4) Churn the fennel-lemon mixture in an ice cream maker, following manufacturer's instructions.

INGREDIENTS

1 fennel bulb, about 3/4 pound
3/4 cup fresh of lemon juice, strained
3/4 cup of sugar

---

(5) While it is churning, chop 2 tablespoons reserved fennel leaves, taking care to exclude tough stems. Fold leaves into the sorbet just as it has finished freezing but is still soft.

(6) Let the sorbet, covered tightly, ripen in the freezer for a few hours before serving.

NOTE: Lemon skin halves, scraped clean and frozen, make decorative containers for a scoop of sorbet.

MAKES 1 SCANT QUART

LEMON SORBET

NOTE: One of the first ices ever made, lemon sorbet is still as refreshing as an ocean breeze on a summer's day.

(1) Make a simple syrup by heating water and sugar in a saucepan, stirring until the sugar is dissolved. Don't cook it any longer because it will start to caramelize and the flavor will change. Add the lemon peel. Take off heat and let it infuse.
(2) When it's cool add the lemon juice. Chill, preferably overnight.
(3) Before you freeze the sorbet, taste it. If the flavor is too intense, stir in up to a half-cup of water to taste. Whisk the egg white to a light froth, and set it aside.
(4) Strain sorbet mixture, pour it into your ice cream maker and follow manufacturer's instructions.
(5) When it's half done, add the frothy egg white. Finish churning.
(6) Store tightly covered in container in the freezer.
(7) Serve garnished with fresh mint and a sprinkle of grated lemon peel.

◈ INGREDIENTS

2 cups of water
2 cups of sugar
1/2 cup lemon peel, more or less (plus some for garnish, if you like)
1 cup of fresh squeezed lemon juice (You'll need 3 or 4 lemons.)
1 egg white
fresh mint for garnish (optional)

MAKES ONE QUART

VODKA OPTION

2 tablespoons lemon-flavored vodka

NOTE: Instead of adding an egg white to the sorbet as it churns, pour in the vodka. Like the egg it will keep the sorbet scoopably soft, and it will add a little zip as well.

MANGO SORBET

NOTE: Accentuate the tropical flavor of mangoes by serving this garnished with slices of lime, kiwi, or both.

(1) Combine water and sugar in a saucepan over medium heat.
(2) Stir occasionally until sugar is completely dissolved. Just as it comes to the boiling point, remove from heat and let cool.
(3) Stir puréed mango and lime juice into sugar syrup and chill in refrigerator, preferably overnight.
(4) Churn in your ice cream maker, following manufacturer's instructions.
(5) When it's nearly done, blend in the rum.
(6) Store tightly covered in container in your freezer.

INGREDIENTS

1 cup of water
3/4 cup of sugar
2 cups of puréed mango. (Use fresh mangoes or unsweetened frozen chunks, thawed.)
3/4 cup of fresh lime juice
3 tablespoons of rum

MAKES ONE QUART

ORANGE SORBET

NOTE: If anything can make a gray winter's day sunny, it's a bowl of orange sorbet. 18th-century chef, Mr Borella, recommended adding lemon juice because "it will fatten the sugar and make your ices more mellow." It's true, it makes the sorbet burst with freshness.

(1) Pour water into a saucepan, add sugar and cook, stirring, over medium heat until the sugar is dissolved.
(2) Add the orange peel. Take off the heat and let the flavors infuse while it cools.
(3) Combine orange and lemon juices.
(4) When the sugar syrup has cooled, stir it into the juices.
(5) Strain into a clean bowl and refrigerate until cold, preferably overnight.
(6) Pour the chilled mixture into your ice cream maker, and churn according to manufacturer's instructions.
(7) Transfer to containers and put in freezer to firm up.

INGREDIENTS

1 cup of water
1 cup of sugar
1/3 cup sliced orange peel
2 cups of freshly squeezed orange juice (from about 4 or 5 oranges)
2 tablespoons of freshly squeezed lemon juice

MAKES ONE QUART

CANDY OPTION
2 tablespoons finely chopped, candied peel

Add the candied peel to the sorbet just before it's done churning. Or simply sprinkle some over the sorbet when it's served. Stores that specialize in nuts, often in Middle Eastern neighborhoods, sometimes have freshly candied peel. Too often the stuff you get at the grocery store is old and tasteless.

PEPPERY PINEAPPLE SORBET

NOTE: *The heat of freshly ground pepper is a nice counterpoint to the lush sweetness of pineapple. This is attractive served in the scooped-out halves of the pineapple.*

(1) Combine sugar and water in a saucepan, and cook, stirring, over medium heat until the sugar is dissolved. Set aside to cool.

(2) Core and cut the pineapples into chunks. Purée in a food processor. Measure. If you have more than you need, use the extra for something else. If you have a little less, add a bit of water.

(4) Mix puréed pineapple with cooled sugar syrup and stir in lemon juice. Chill in refrigerator, preferably overnight.

(5) Pour the mixture into your ice cream maker and churn according to manufacturer's instructions.

(6) Just before it's ready, grind the pepper and mix it in.

(7) Serve or store in containers in your freezer.

INGREDIENTS

1 cup of sugar
1 cup of water
1 pineapple (2 1/2 cups of purée)
1 tablespoon fresh lemon juice
1 teaspoon of freshly ground black pepper

MAKES ONE QUART

RUM OPTION

2 tablespoons rum

Add to the sorbet when you mix in the ground pepper.

RASPBERRY SORBET

NOTE: Fresh, not dried, rosemary gives the flavor an edge and makes it memorable. Escoffier paired peaches and raspberries in his Peach Melba. In homage, slice fresh peaches in half, remove the stones and fill with a scoop of raspberry sorbet. Garnish with a sprig of rosemary.

(1) Pour water into a saucepan, add sugar and cook, stirring, over medium heat until the sugar dissolves.

(2) Mix the lemon juice and rosemary into the sugar syrup and let them infuse until you can taste them in the syrup.

(3) Purée the berries in a blender or food processor and measure. You should have 2 cups.

(4) Blend with the sugar syrup. Strain. Chill thoroughly.

(5) Churn in your ice cream maker, according to manufacturer's instructions.

(6) Store tightly covered in a container in your freezer.

◼ INGREDIENTS

4 cups of fresh raspberries (unsweetened frozen berries are an okay substitute)
1 cup of water
1 cup of sugar
2 tablespoons of fresh lemon juice
1 tablespoon of roughly chopped, fresh rosemary

MAKES ONE QUART

SPARKLING SLUSH

NOTE: This is not for your best bottle of Champagne. Rather, use a flavorful, fruity bubbly or, if there is such a thing available, leftover sparkling wine. Fresh strawberries are a natural partner, as are crisp wafer cookies.

(1) Pour water into a saucepan, add sugar and cook, stirring, over medium heat until the sugar dissolves.
(2) Let cool and mix with the wine and lemon juice. Chill.
(3) Churn in your ice cream maker, according to manufacturer's instructions.
(4) Store tightly covered in a container in your freezer.

NOTE: Because of the alcohol, this won't get completely firm right away. It needs a few hours or overnight in a container in your freezer. It will also melt quickly once it's served. But like most fleeting pleasures, it's wonderful while it lasts.

INGREDIENTS

1 cup of sugar
1 cup of water
2 1/2 cups of sparkling wine
1 tablespoon of lemon juice

MAKES ONE QUART

TARRAGON & ORANGE SORBET

NOTE: Tarragon's clean, herbal flavor is perfect in a sorbet. Orange peel gives it a little edge. The combination is recommended by Alice Arndt in her book Seasoning Savvy, *The Haworth Herbal Press, and it's now one of my favorites.*

(1) Pour two cups of water into a saucepan, add sugar and cook over medium heat until the sugar dissolves.
(2) Stir in the tarragon and orange peel. Remove from heat, and let them infuse until the mixture cools.
(3) Add the other cup of water.
(4) Chill in refrigerator, preferably overnight.
(5) Lightly whisk egg white and set aside.
(6) Strain sorbet mixture, and then churn in your ice cream maker, according to manufacturer's instructions.
(7) When it's almost done, mix in the egg white.
(8) Store tightly covered in container in your freezer.

▣ INGREDIENTS

2 cups of water
1 1/2 cups of sugar
2 tablespoons of roughly chopped, fresh tarragon (don't use dried)
2 tablespoons of roughly chopped orange peel
1 cup of water
1 egg white

MAKES ONE QUART

TEA SORBET

NOTE: If you like iced tea, you'll like tea ice. Strongly flavored teas work best - mint flavored, Red Zinger, Earl Grey. The rum enhances the flavor, and helps keep the sorbet scoopable.

(1) Pour water into a saucepan, add sugar and cook, stirring, over medium heat until the sugar dissolves.
(2) Brew the tea and strain loose tea or discard bags.
(3) Combine tea, sugar syrup and lemon juice. Chill thoroughly.
(4) Churn in your ice cream maker, according to manufacturer's instructions.
(5) When it's nearly done, mix in the rum.
(6) Store tightly covered in container in your freezer.

ICED TEA, TOO

Serve a scoop of tea sorbet in a glass of iced tea for twice the flavor.

INGREDIENTS

2/3 cup of sugar
1 cup of water
2 1/2 cups of strong tea. (Use 5 tea bags, or the equivalent in loose tea.)
1 tablespoon of lemon juice
2 tablespoons of rum

MAKES ONE QUART

GRANITA

NOTE: You don't need an ice cream freezer to make a wonderful granita. Just mix the ingredients together, pour the mixture into a shallow pan and put it in the freezer. As it freezes, scrape the ice crystals with a fork from time to time. It's not as time consuming as it sounds because it takes just a minute each time you scrape the mixture. When it's done, the ice will have the finely granulated texture that gives granita its name.

CAMPARI & SODA GRANITA

Campari and soda is not a traditional granita but it is a classic Italian aperitif and a fabulous one when iced. It's also a refreshing summer dessert.

(1) In a saucepan over medium heat, combine water and sugar and cook, stirring, until sugar has dissolved. Set aside to cool.

(2) Mix cooled syrup with lime juice, Campari and soda. Taste to make sure it's strong enough. Add a little more Campari if necessary. It should taste slightly too strong, since it will be milder when it's frozen.

(3) Pour the mixture into an 8-inch square pan and put it in the freezer.

(4) When it's icy around the edges, use a fork to scrape the icy crystals from the edges of the pan, breaking them into the smallest possible grains.

(5) Repeat every half hour or so until the entire mixture consists of small grains of frozen Campari and soda.

(6) Serve or store in a plastic container in your freezer.
(7) Just before you serve it. fluff up the grains with a fork again. It's best to make this on the same day you plan to serve it but it will keep for another day or two.
(8) Garnish it with a wedge of lime.

▨ INGREDIENTS

1 cup of water
2/3 cup of sugar
2 tablespoons of lime juice
1/2 cup of Campari
3/4 cup of club soda
lime wedge for garnish

SERVES 4

ESPRESSO GRANITA

NOTE: Espresso granita *is traditional and very versatile. Serve in cups and top with softly whipped cream. Or alternate layers of espresso* granita *and whipped cream in tall glasses. It's also very nice served with coffee, hazelnut or almond-flavored liqueur poured over it.*

(1) Brew the coffee. If you have an espresso maker, use it. If not, just brew according to your usual method but make it a little stronger than you ordinarily would.

(2) Stir in sugar to dissolve. Taste and add more sugar if necessary.

(3) Add lemon peel. Let the mixture cool, then strain it.

(4) Pour the coffee into a shallow pan, large enough so the liquid isn't more than an inch deep. An 8-inch square pan works well.

(5) Freeze until it's icy around the edges. Then, using a fork, scrape the icy crystals from the edges of the pan breaking them into the smallest possible grains. Repeat every half hour or so until the entire mixture consists of small grains of frozen coffee.

(6) Serve or store in a plastic container in your freezer.

▧ INGREDIENTS

2 8-ounce cups of brewed espresso or strong coffee (Use decaf if coffee keeps you awake and you plan to serve this after dinner.)
1/4 cup of sugar
a slice of lemon peel

---

(7) Just before you serve it, fluff up the grains with a fork again. It's best to make this on the same day you plan to serve it but it will keep for another day or so.

SERVES 4

SAUCES

BLACKBERRY SAUCE

NOTE: Not only is this terrific on ices and ice cream, especially the almond ice on page 29, it's also a wonderful pancake or waffle topping. Boston-area food writer Roz Cummins came up with it.

(1) Combine berries, sugar, and lemon juice, and heat in a pot on the stove or in a microwave-safe covered bowl in the microwave until the berries are soft, and they have given off a lot of juice. (four to five minutes on high power in the microwave if using frozen berries)

(2) Stir in vanilla extract and cinnamon. Taste and add more sugar if you like.

(3) Force berry mixture through a sieve. If you want a smoother sauce, purée it in a blender or food processor.

(4) Serve warm.

INGREDIENTS

1 1/2 cups of fresh blackberries (or a 10-ounce bag of unsweetened frozen blackberries)
2/3 to 3/4 cup of sugar (to taste)
1 tablespoon of lemon juice
1/4 teaspoon of vanilla extract
1/4 teaspoon of cinnamon

SERVES 8

CARAMEL SAUCE

NOTE: Great with chocolate ice cream, caramel sauce is also terrific with the Five Spice Cream on page 50.

(1) Combine sugar and water in a heavy-bottomed saucepan and cook over medium heat until the mixture turns a light amber. Be very careful. Molten sugar will burn you badly.

(2) Meanwhile, warm cream in a container with a pour spout. A glass measuring cup works well, and it takes only a minute in the microwave. Set aside.

(3) When the sugar is ready, take it off the heat and add the butter. Then gently pour in the cream. It will probably froth up angrily, so stand back. Stir carefully. Add the salt.

(4) Let it cool, then store in a glass jar in the refrigerator.

(5) It may firm up when cold, but a 30-second zap in the microwave will make it pourable.

▣ INGREDIENTS

1 cup of sugar
1/4 cup of water
1 tablespoon of butter
1/2 cup of heavy cream
pinch of salt

BUTTERSCOTCH SAUCE

NOTE: When I was a kid, a butterscotch sundae with coffee ice cream was one of my favorites. It still is.

(1) Combine sugar, corn syrup, butter and salt in a saucepan over medium heat.
(2) Bring to a simmer and cook, stirring occasionally, for about five minutes.
(3) Remove from heat and let it cool slightly. Stir in the cream and vanilla.
(4) Store in a glass jar in the refrigerator.
(5) It may firm up when cold, but a 30-second zap in the microwave will have it pouring again.

▩ INGREDIENTS

1 cup of light brown sugar
1/3 cup of light corn syrup
4 tablespoons of butter
pinch of salt
1/2 cup of heavy cream
1/2 teaspoon of vanilla

CHOCOLATE SAUCE

NOTE: A classic poured over vanilla, this is a taste revelation on ginger or chestnut or caramel ice creams.

(1) Warm cream in a saucepan and add chocolate, sugar and butter. Cook, stirring, over very low heat for about 10 minutes.
(2) Remove from heat and stir in the vanilla and salt.
(3) If you're not using it right away, cool and then store in a glass jar in the refrigerator.
(4) It will firm up when cold, but a 30-second zap in the microwave will make it pourable again.

INGREDIENTS

1/3 cup of heavy cream
4 ounces of bittersweet chocolate, or 1/2 cup of chocolate chips
1/4 cup of sugar
2 tablespoons of butter
1/2 teaspoon of vanilla
pinch of salt

GRAND CHOCOLATE SAUCE

Substitute 2 tablespoons of Grand Marnier for the vanilla.

COFFEE SYRUP

NOTE: Serve this intensely flavored syrup with any of the coffee-flavored ices or ice creams for a double whammy. It's great with the Mocha Ice Cream on page 56.

(1) Pour coffee and sugar into a saucepan and cook over low heat until the mixture reduces and becomes syrupy.
(2) Take off the heat and let it cool slightly.
(3) Stir in the salt and vanilla.
(4) Pour into a glass jar and store in refrigerator.

INGREDIENTS

1 1/2 8-ounce measuring cups of freshly brewed coffee
1 cup of sugar
Pinch of salt
1/2 teaspoon of vanilla

SIMPLE SERVINGS

NOTE: Whether you use the ice creams in this book or ones you've bought, here are some splendid and east ways to serve them.

GELATO AFFOGATO

I once tried to order an iced coffee in Italy and was served this delightful dessert. I later learned that it's called *gelato affogato*, which means 'drowned ice cream.' Sometimes, not being fluent in a language can turn out to be an advantage.

❖ INGREDIENTS
espresso
vanilla ice cream

Simply puddle some warm, freshly brewed espresso around a scoop or two of the best vanilla ice cream you can buy or, of course, make. It's a fabulous combination.

LAKE COMO ICE CREAM

On an island on Italy's Lake Como there is an inn and restaurant called *Locanda dell'Isola Comacina*. The chef prepares this simple dessert out on the terrace as sunlight sparkles on the lake waters. The dish is not as scenic at home, but it is as delectable.

INGREDIENTS
fresh oranges
vanilla ice cream
banana liqueur

> For each serving, use half an orange. Peel oranges with a knife so there's no pith left. Then cut oranges horizontally into thin slices. Arrange orange slices on a dish, top with a scoop or two of vanilla ice cream. Then pour a little banana liqueur over it all. The whole is much more than the parts.

ICE CREAM WITH CANDIED CHESTNUTS

> When you want to serve an sophisticated dessert, but don't have time to make one, this is an elegant solution.

INGREDIENTS
jarred, candied chestnuts in brandy
vanilla or chocolate ice cream
whipped cream

> Simply top the ice cream with chestnuts and softly whipped cream. Add a little brandy to the cream for an even more tempting serving. Use candied ginger in syrup instead of chestnuts for different treats.

HOT CHOCOLATE GROWS UP

How to turn a simple childhood treat into an elegant dessert for all ages.

▩ INGREDIENTS
hot chocolate
coffee ice cream
Whipped cream and cinnamon

> Make your hot chocolate as usual. Then plop a scoop of ice cream in each cup, top with whipped cream and dust with cinnamon.

CANNOLI CONES

Turn cannoli shells into ice cream cones for a change-of-pace dessert.

▩ INGREDIENTS
cannoli shells
ice cream
pistachio nuts

> Buy cannoli shells and fill them with your favorite ice cream, then dip the ends in finely chopped pistachios.

SHELL GAMES

Serve ices and ice creams in the scooped-out shells of fruits such as lemons, oranges, pineapples, melons or kiwi. You can freeze the empty shells first, to help them keep their shape, and to provide a suitable chilly container.

FLAVORED WHIPPED CREAMS

Top your ice cream with a different cream. Instead of adding vanilla to whipped cream, try other flavored extracts such as orange, lemon, or almond.

Or add a little cocoa for a chocolate whipped cream.

Crush a few strawberries and strain the juice into your cream, then top with fresh strawberries.

Or whip the cream with a tablespoon or so of a dessert liqueur like Grand Marnier or Frangelico.

SWIRLS, SPRINKLES & ADD-INS

Don't stop with chocolate sprinkles, try some of these atop, around or swirled through your ice cream.

Angostura Bitters

You've probably got a bottle in the back of your liquor cabinet. Take it out and pour a little over vanilla, orange, coffee or other ice creams.

Quince Paste

Its intense orange color and tart-sweet flavor are wonderful mixed into vanilla ice cream. You'll find quince paste in Middle Eastern markets or the gourmet section of grocery stores.

Nutella

Now widely available, this Italian hazelnut and chocolate paste is great swirled into chocolate, coffee or vanilla ice creams.

Jam

Swirl raspberry jam into vanilla, strawberry jam into pistachio.

Crushed Peppermint Sticks

Smash up some candy canes, mix them into ice cream, and surprise the kids with a treat they'll love.

TOPPINGS

Crushed *amaretti* cookies
Crushed praline or nut brittles
Shaved chocolate
Sifted cinnamon and/or nutmeg
Sifted cocoa
Slivers of candied ginger
Sweet liqueurs
Toasted coconut
Toasted, chopped nuts
Toasted pine nuts

INDEX

Alcohol.. 16, 17, 28, 85
    brandy.. 97
    Champagne
        in Sparkling Slush..................... 85
    orange liqueur (Grand Marnier)
        in Orange Marmalade Ice
        Cream...60
    Port
        in Cantaloupe & Port Sorbet.....74
    rum
        in Banana Daiquiri Ice Cream....33
        in Chestnut Rum Raisin.............38
        in Pina Colada Ice Cream..........61
        in Biscuit Tortoni.......................69
        in Mango Sorbet........................80
        in Tea Sorbet............................87
    sherry
        in Oloroso Ice Cream................58
    vodka, lemon flavored, as option................79
almond extract...28
    in Almond Ice Cream........................30, 31
    in Cranberry-Pistachio Ice Cream............47
    in Pistachio Ice Cream 62
    in Almond Sorbet.....................................73
ALMOND ICE CREAM............................. 30, 31, 64
ALMOND SORBET... 73
almond syrup.. 73
almonds 18
    in Almond Ice Cream........................30,31
    in Royal Ice Cream...................................65
amaretti cookies
    in Biscuit Tortoni..................................... 69
    crushed..101
American Cookery..10
Angostura Bitters 100

Anheuser-Busch... 19
APPLE SAUCE ICE CREAM 32
apples
    in Apple Sauce Ice Cream................32
    baked..76
Arndt, Alice... 86
arrowroot... 10
artichoke, as flavor for ice cream...................... 8
Babe Ruth.. 20
banana
    in Banana Daiquiri Ice Cream..............33
BANANA DAIQUIRI ICE CREAM..................27, 33
banana liqueur
    in Pina Colada Ice Cream................... 97
Baskin-Robbins.. 22
Ben & Jerry's.. 24
BISCUIT TORTONI................................... 27, 69
bittersweet or semisweet chocolate
    in Chocolate Hazelnut Ice Cream..............41
    in Coconut Chocolate Chip Ice Cream.....45
black pepper
    in Peppery Pineapple Sorbet......................82
blackberries
    in Blackberry Sauce...................................91
BLACKBERRY SAUCE 73, 91
blueberries
    in Cinnamon Blueberry Swirl........... 42, 43
Borella..65, 81
Brillat-Savarin... 3
butter....................................... .10, 24, 50, 92, 93, 94
butterfat... 23, .24
BUTTERSCOTCH SAUCE 93
Campari
    in Campari & Soda Granita.....................88
CAMPARI & SODA GRANITA...............................88

candied citron 6
candy canes .... .100
cannoli shells 98
Cantaloupe
    in Cantaloupe & Port Sorbet 74
CANTALOUPE & PORT SORBET 74
CARAMEL ICE CREAM 34
CARAMEL SAUCE 92
CARDAMOM ORANGE ICE CREAM 35
cardamom pods
    in Cardamom Orange Ice Cream 35
Catherine de Medici 4
Champagne
    in Sparkling Slush 85
Charlie Chaplin 20
cheeses, Parmesan and Gruyère (as flavoring) 8
CHERRIES JUBILEE 36
cherries
    dried tart, in Cherries Jubilee 36
CHESTNUT RUM RAISIN ICE CREAM .... .38
chestnuts 97
    in Chestnut Rum Raisin Ice Cream 38
CHOCOLATE HAZELNUT ICE CREAM 40
CHOCOLATE MOUSSE 70
CHOCOLATE SAUCE 94
CHOCOLATE SORBET A L'EMY 75
CHOCOLATE SPICE CREAM 39
chocolate
    bittersweet
        as Cherries Jubilee option 37
        in Chocolatee Hazelnut 40
        in Chocolate Spice Cream 39
        in Chocolate Sorbet 75
        in Chocolate Sauce 94
    hot 98

semi-sweet
        as Cherries Jubilee option 37
        in Chocolatee Mousse 70
        in Chocolate Sauce 71
cholesterol 25
cinnamon 6, 32, 39, 42, 43, 63, 75, 76, 91, 98, 101
    in Cinnamon Blueberry Swirl Ice Cream 42
    in Cinnamon Ice 76
CINNAMON BLUEBERRY SWIRL ICE CREAM 42
CINNAMON ICE A LA LATINI 76
cinnamon stick
    in Cinnamon Blueberry Swirl Ice Cream 43
    in Cinnamon Ice 76
citron peel
    in Royal Ice Cream 65
cloves
    ground 32 39, 63, 75, 76
club soda
    in Compari & Soda Granita 89
cocoa
    sifted, as garnish 101
    unsweetened, in Chocolate Sorbet 75
    unsweetened Dutch process, in Mocha Ice
        Cream 57
COCONUT CHOCOLATE CHIP ICE CREAM .. 44
coconut milk
    in Coconut Chocolate Chip 44, 45
    in Pina Colada Ice Cream 61
coffee 24, 46, 56, 57, 68, 73, 90, 93, 95, 96, 98, 100
    in Coffee Ice Cream ....
    in White Coffee Ice Cream 68
COFFEE ICE CREAM 46
coffee beans 46, 56, 57, 68
cone 18, 19
Confectioners' Journal 14

coriander
    ground, in Royal Ice Cream 65
corn syrup
    in Butterscotch Sauce 93
cranberries
    in Cranberry Pistachio Ice Cream 47
CRANBERRY-PISTACHIO ICE Cream 47
cream ices 6
Creamsicle 18
CREME DE PROVENCE 48
cucumber sorbet 16
Cummins, Roz 39, 91
cupcake tins (for mousse) 70
custard 11, 16, 27, 28, 44, 46
Dairy Queen 22
Disneyland 23
Dixie cup 22
Dolley Madison 9
"drowned ice cream" 96
EARL GREY'S ICE CREAM 49
Emy 5, 8, 25, 68, 75
Escoffier 8, 84
Eskimo pie 18
espresso
    in Coffee Ice Cream 46
    in Espresso Granita 90
    in Gelato Affogato 96
espresso beans, Chocolate Covered 46
ESPRESSO GRANITA 90
fennel
    as flavoring 6, 77
FENNEL LEMON SORBET 77
Five Spice powder 50
FIVE-SPICE CREAM 50
FLAVORED WHIPPED CREAMS 99

FROZEN MOUSSES 69
Frozen Puddings and Desserts 16
Fudgsicle 18
Fussell, Jacob 12
gelatin 16
GELATO AFFOGATO 96
gianduja 40
GINGER - GINGER ICE CREAM 52
ginger,
    fresh, in Ginger-Ginger Ice Cream 52
    ground, in Pumpkin Praline Ice Cream 63
Good Humor bar 18
Grand Marnier 60, 71, 94, 99
GRANITAS 88
    CAMPARI & SODA GRANITA 88
    ESPRESSO GRANITA 90
H.P. Hood Company 22
Häagen-Dazs 24
Hamwi, Ernest 18
hazelnuts
    in Chocolate Hazelnut Ice Cream 40, 41
Heath bar 24
Herrell, Steve 24
honey 4
    in Creme de Provence 48

Hoodsie 22
HOT CHOCOLATE GROWS UP 98
Howard Johnson's 22
ice cream maker, instructions for 26
ice cream parlor 19, 21, 23
ice cream sandwich 18
ice cream soda 17
ice crystals 27, 88
ice harvesters 12

iced creams 6
ices 2, 4, 6, 8, 9, 12, 16, 18, 19, 78, 81, 91
jam, as flavoring 60, 100
Jefferson, Thomas 9
Johnson, Nancy 12
Kirsch
       in Cherries Jubilee 36
LAKE COMO ICE CREAM 96
Latini, Antonio 4, 6, 76
lavender
       in Creme de Provence 48
lemon 6, 8, 10, 16, 19, 32, 54, 55, 58, 60, 64, 65, 73, 75, 76, 77, 78, 79, 81, 82, 84, 85, 87, 90, 91, 99
lemon extract 54, 55
LEMON ICE CREAM 54
lemon juice 32, 54, 60, 64, 73, 76, 77, 78, 81, 82, 84, 85, 87, 91
lemon peel
       in Oloroso Ice Cream 58
       in Royal Ice Cream 65
       in Chocolate Sorbet 75
       in Lemon Sorbet 78
       as Garnish for Espresso Granita 90
LEMON SORBET 78
Lenzi, Philip 10
lime juice
       in Banana Dacquiri Ice Cream 33
       in Mango Sorbet 80
       in Campari & Soda Granita 88, 89
Locanda dell'Isola Comacina 96
M. Emy (see Emy)
Madison, Dolley 9
mango
       in Mango Sorbet 80
MANGO SORBET 80

MAPLE PECAN MOUSSE 72
maple syrup
       in Maple Pecan Mousse 72
Marchiony, Italo 19
Marco Polo 3
marmalade, Seville orange
       in Orange Marmalade Ice Cream 60
Marshall, Agnes 18
Martineau, Harriet 11
Masters, Thomas 12
Mattus, Reuben 24
mint, fresh, as garnish for Lemon Sorbet 78
mocha, definition of 56
MOCHA ICE CREAM 56
Moka 56
molds for ices and ice creams 7, 19
molto buono 40
MOUSSES, FROZEN 69- 72
       Biscuit Tortoni 69
       Chocolate Mousse 70
       Maple Pecan Mousse 72
Neapolitan Ice Cream 16
New York Gazette 10
Nutella, as flavoring 100
nutmeg
       in Apple Sauce Ice Cream 32
       in Pumpkin Praline Ice Cream 63
Oloroso Sherry
       in Oloroso Ice Cream 58
OLOROSO ICE CREAM 58
orange, as flavoring 8, 16, 22
orange extract
       in Cardamom Orange Ice Cream 35
       in Creme de Provence 48
orange flower water 59

    in Orange Flower Water Ice Cream...........59
ORANGE FLOWER WATER ICE CREAM...........59
orange juice
    in Strawberry Rhubarb Ice Cream..............66
    in Cantaloupe & Port Sorbet.....................74
    in Orange Sorbet 81
orange liqueur (Grand Marnier)
    in Orange Marmalade Ice Cream...............60
    in Grand Chocolate Sauce.........................94
ORANGE MARMALADE ICE CREAM............... 60
orange peel
    in Cardamom Orange Ice Cream...............35
    in Creme de Provence................................48
    in Oloroso Ice Cream................................58
    in Orange Sorbet.......................................81
    in Tarragon and Orange Sorbet................ 86
ORANGE SORBET..81
oranges, fresh, for Orange Sorbet........................ 81
Oreo cookies.. 24
oyster, as flavoring...10
parfaites... 8
Parloa, Maria.. 12
Peach Melba.. 84
pecans
    in Pumpkin Praline Ice Cream..................63
    in Maple Pecan Mousse.............................72
penny licks... 18
peppermint sticks, crushed 100
pepper
    in Peppery Pineapple Sorbet......................82
PEPPERY PINEAPPLE SORBET 82
PINA COLADA ICE CREAM 61
pine nuts
    in Oloroso Ice Cream................................58
    in Cinnamon Ice A La Latini....................76

    as topping..101
pineapple
    as flavoring.......................................16, 61, 82
    in Peppery Pineapple Sorbet..................... 82
    in Pina Colada Ice Cream..........................61
pistachio
    as flavoring........................ 6, 47, 62, 98, 100
    in Cranberry Pistachio Ice Cream..............47
    in Pistachio Ice Cream...............................62
PISTACHIO ICE CREAM 62
plantations... 11
Popsicle 18
Port
    in Cantaloupe & Port Sorbet.................... 74
Prohibition 19
pumpkin, as flavoring................................ 6, 63, 67
    in Pumpkin Praline Ice Cream 63
PUMPKIN PRALINE ICE CREAM 63
quince paste, as flavoring... 100
raisins
    in Apple Sauce Ice Cream.........................32
    in Chestnut Rum Raisin Ice Cream...........38
    in Oloroso Ice Cream................................58
Randolph, Mary 10
raspberries
    in Raspberry Ice Cream............................. 64
    in Raspberry Sorbet...................................84
RASPBERRY ICE CREAM 64
RASPBERY SORBET 84
Reese's Peanut Butter Cups................................... 24
Refrigeration 6, 12, 20-21
rhubarb
    in Strawberry-Rhubarb Ice Cream.............66
Riely, Elizabeth... 77
Roaring Twenties... 19

Roosevelt, Franklin D. 20
Rorer, Sarah.. 16
rosemary
    fresh, in Raspberry Sorbet........................ 84
ROYAL ICE CREAM 65
rum 33, 38, 61, 69, 80, 83, 87
rum
    in Banana Dacquiri Ice Cream...................33
    in Chestnut Rum Raisin..............................38
    in Pina Colada Ice Cream...........................61
    in Biscuit Tortoni...69
    in Mango Sorbet..80
    in Tea Sorbet...87
SAUCES(for ice cream) 91-95
    BLACKBERRY SAUCE 91
    BUTTERSCOTCH SAUCE......................93
    CARAMEL SAUCE...................................92
    CHOCOLATE SAUCE..............................94
    GRAND CHOCOLATE SAUCE.............94
sharbât 4
sherry
    in Oloroso Ice Cream..................................58
Side-Walk Sundae..20
Simmons, Amelia.. 10
soda fountain 17, 19, 23
sorbet 4, 16, 73, 74, 75, 76, 77, 78, 79, 80, 81, 82, 83, 84, 86, 87
sorbetière 7
SORBETS 73-88
    ALMOND SORBET..................................73
    CANTALOUPE & PORT SORBET........74
    CHOCOLATE SORBET A L'EMY..........75
    CINNAMON ICE A LA LATINI............76
    FENNEL LEMON SORBET.....................77
    LEMON SORBET.......................................78

MANGO SORBET......................................80
ORANGE SORBET....................................81
PEPPERY PINEAPPLE SORBET..............82
RASPBERRY SORBET...............................84
SPARKLING SLUSH.................................85
TARRAGON & ORANGE SORBET.....86
TEA SORBET..87
sorbetto 4
SPARKLING SLUSH... 85
sprinkles 100
Steve's 24
strawberries
    as flavoring or garnish..............18, 66, 85, 99
    in Strawberry-Rhubarb Ice Cream.............66
STRAWBERRY-RHUBARB ICE CREAM 66
sugar, brown
    inPumpkin Praline Ice Cream.................. 63
    in Butterscotch Sauce.................................93
sugar, confectioner's
    in Biscuit Tortoni..69
superpremium 24, 25
swirls 100
TARRAGON & ORANGE SORBET..................... 86
tarragon
    fresh, in Tarragon & Orange Sorbet........ 86
Tastee Freeze 22
tea
    as flavoring...................................... 6, 49, 87
    in Earl Grey's Ice Cream............................49
    in Tea Sorbet...87
TEA SORBET..87
Thanksgiving 63, 105
The Depression 20
The Virginia House-wife 10
Thoreau, Henry David... 12

tomato sorbet 16
vanilla beans 67
VANILLA PLAIN & PERFECT 67
vendors, ice cream 14
Victory Sundaes 22
vodka, lemon-flavored... 79
walnuts, as flavoring... 8, 53
Washington, George 9
whipped cream............................. 70, 72, 90, 97, 98, 99
WHITE COFFEE ICE CREAM 68
White Sulphur Springs, Virginia.................................. 11
Wilder, Thornton.. 29
wine, sparkling
       in Sparkling Slush.......................................85
World's Fair 18

NOTES

Traditional Country Life Recipe Books from
BRICK TOWER PRESS

For sales, editorial information, subsidiary rights information or a catalog, please write or phone or e-mail to the appropriate address below:

Brick Tower Press
1230 Park Avenue
New York, NY 10128, US
Sales: 1-800-68-BRICK
Tel: 212-427-7139 Fax: 212-860-8852
www.BrickTowerPress.com • bookmanuscript.com
cyberbookworks.com
email: bricktower@aol.com.

For Canadian sales please contact our distributor,
Vanwell Publishing Ltd.
1 Northrup Crescent, Box 2131
St. Catharines, ON L2R 7S2
Tel: 905-937-3100

For sales in the UK and Europe please contact our distributor,
Gazelle Book Services
Falcon House, White Cross Mills, Hightown
Lancaster, LA1 4XS, UK
Tel: (01524) 68765 Fax: (01524) 63232
email: sales@gazellebooks.co.uk.

For Australian and New Zealand sales please contact
INT Press Distribution Pyt. Ltd.
386 Mt. Alexander Road
Ascot Vale, VIC 3032, Australia
Tel: 61-3-9326 2416 Fax: 61-3-9326 2413
email: sales@intpress.com.au.

Forthcoming titles:

Pie Companion
Bakery Companion
Salmon Companion
Honey
American Indian Recipes

MAIL ORDER AND GENERAL INFORMATION

Many of our titles are carried by your local book store or gift and museum shop. If they do not already carry our line please ask them to write us for information.

If you are unable to purchase our titles from your local shop, call or write to us. Our titles are available through mail order. Just send us a check or money order for $9.95 per title with $1.50 postage (shipping is free with 3 or more assorted copies) to the Park Avenue address in the adjacent column or call us Monday through Friday, 9 AM to 5 PM, EST. We accept Visa, Mastercard, and American Express cards.

Other titles in this series:

American Chef's Companion
Chocolate Companion
Fresh Herb Companion
Thanksgiving Cookery
Victorian Christmas Cookery
Apple Companion
Pumpkin Companion
Soups, Stews & Chowders
Fresh Bread Companion
Sandwich Companion
Farmstand-Vegetables
Cranberry Companion
Adorable Zucchini